ADVANCE PRAISE FOR *THE PARLAY EFFECT*

Whether you are a woman who supports women, or a man taking the lead in pulling women forward, this book is a must-read.

— **Jocelyn Mangan,** CEO and founder, Him for Her

"The Parlay Effect" is real. When women can contribute their voice assertively and authentically, they move mountains. Anne has opened up a new channel for change.

— **Andy Cunningham,** marketer of innovation and
founder of Cunningham Collective

The Parlay Effect *is going to be my go-to gift for all of the important women, and men, in my life. It is chock-full of inspiration as we all seek deeper meaning in our lives.*

— **Joanna Rees,** managing partner, West

Anne Devereux-Mills has written an endearingly frank and searingly honest account of how the challenges of her own personal journey led her to these revelations, learnings and insights. If you want to change your life, and in doing so, set "the Parlay Effect" in motion to ensure you also impact the lives of many others for the better, read this book!

— **Cindy Gallop,** founder, Make Love Not Porn

As Anne points out in this wonderful book, "We are all stronger when we are connected." A wonderful read, The Parlay Effect *outlines a step-by-step process that works.*

— **Christina Mace-Turner,** founder and CEO, Mab & Stoke

One Small Thing™ is a poignant and persuasive reminder for women of the transformative power of diversity and connection. A moving and inspiring guide to reigniting our sense of purpose and passion.

— **Sherrilyn Ifill,** president, NAACP Legal Defense Fund

*What could be better than women supporting women? Anne Devereux-Mills'
new book,* The Parlay Effect, *shows the power and importance of women
getting together and connecting in meaningful ways. It's the perfect antidote
for the increasingly disconnected time in which we live.*

— **Nina Vaca,** chairman and CEO, The Pinnacle Group

*I love that this book tells one woman's whole story after she pulls back
the curtain on who she thinks she should be in the midst of losing "it all."
It makes being vulnerable a natural part of life and the most important
tool for true human connection.*

— **Larissa May,** founder, #halfthestory

*As someone who believes in creating communities, I love how Parlay House
brings the most diverse range of women together.*

— **Xochi Birch,** co-founder, The Battery

*It's about time we started talking at a deep and vulnerable level, not only
about our similarities but also about how our unique differences can help
accelerate the integration of empathy and hope during the darkest times.*
The Parlay Effect *does just that.*

— **Wendy Behary,** director, The Cognitive Therapy Center of New Jersey

*If something pisses you off but you don't know how to change it,
read this book!*

— **Nancy Lublin,** founder, Crisis Textline

The Parlay Effect *is a gem! Full of wise nuggets and uplifting moments.
Read it and reinforce that helping others should be a natural way of being.
Warning: Will invoke laughter and tears!*

— **Sue Siegel,** CEO, board member and VC

THE
PARLAY
EFFECT

HOW FEMALE CONNECTION
CAN CHANGE THE WORLD

ANNE DEVEREUX-MILLS

PARLAY HOUSE BOOKS

THE PARLAY EFFECT
How Female Connection Can Change the World

$$\boxed{P}$$

Parlay House Books
San Francisco, California
www.parlayhouse.com

ISBN-978-1-7333959-0-8

Library of Congress Cataloging-in-Publication Data
is available upon request

Book design: Tom Joyce / Creativewerks
Cover: Nikki McDonald
Author's portrait: Jamie Nease
Typeset in Minion Pro and Goldenbook

THE PARLAY EFFECT

To Lauren and Ciara, who lift me,
And to David, who holds me tight.

CONTENTS

par·lay

/ ˈpär, lā /

verb: to increase or otherwise transform
  into something greater.

noun: from the world of gambling, where the stakes
  are higher with cumulative bets.

verb: from the French word *parler,* meaning
  to speak or to talk.

THE SCIENCE BEHIND SMALL ACTIONS

By Serena Chen, Ph.D.

I BECAME INTERESTED IN WORKING WITH ANNE Devereux-Mills on a scientific study of what she had dubbed "the Parlay Effect," because we both care about supporting women and their personal and professional growth. We both believe that this support can extend beyond women themselves to help make their children, families and communities stronger.

When I first met Anne, I felt an immediate connection to her, because we shared not only similar values and interests, but parallel life experiences. We were both mothers, had each gone through a divorce, had time-consuming careers that we cared about, and deeply valued female connection. We both had an interest in diversity and in helping to build a more accepting world by considering ways to increase income equality and equality of access to opportunity. She immediately struck me as a fighter with a lot of hard-won wisdom about people, life and what really matters.

I've been a professor of psychology for over 20 years, and have studied social psychology for nearly 30 years, starting during my undergraduate years at Cornell University. When I went on to get my doctorate in social psychology at New York University, I became interested in topics that I am still studying today: how people define themselves and how the social hierarchy influences our thoughts, feelings and behavior. After NYU, I took my first job as a professor at the University of Michigan in Ann Arbor, and then moved on to the University of California, Berkeley in 2001, where I've been ever since. One major branch of my research for the last 25 years has focused on the social nature of our concepts of self—specifically on how people think about themselves, and how our parents, romantic partners, siblings, friends, co-workers and so on influence who we are. I'm fascinated by the fact that we are deeply social beings, and that who we are is always a reflection of and adaptation to our social environment. This is one of the key aspects of being human, and to truly grasp what drives human behavior, we need to take into account the social context of our everyday lives. In my laboratory, we study how this basic fact helps to illuminate the goals people pursue, how we fare in relationships, the choices we make, and how we deal with failure—and the list goes on. In the past five years, my research on the self has moved toward topics that have a bearing on people's well-being—such as my work on the psychological and relational benefits of self-compassion, as well as authenticity. All of these aspects of society and relationships are reflected in Anne's drive to start Parlay House and to write this book.

The second major branch of my research has focused on studying how one's location in a social hierarchy—for example, whether or not we occupy a position of authority, or are considered to be higher or lower in social status—influences how we interact with one another. The overriding concern driving this research is that differences in social standing can have a deleterious effect on the social fabric, and that it is important to understand these differences and how to overcome them.

Anne approached me with the idea of doing a broader research study to explore the effects of the relationships and actions that she was observing between people who participated in her Parlay House salons. She writes in the introduction to this book: "I saw that the gatherings trigger a series of micro-actions that amplify far beyond our group. One woman finds herself in a position to help another through kindness, empathy, generosity or encouragement, and the woman who received that help then replicates it, passing it on to another woman."

Anne explained to me that she wanted to examine these kinds of actions, the feelings that they aroused, and the "triggers" for the actions that lead to this cascade of positive experiences and change. In talking, we concluded that a research study of the "Parlay Effect" would more broadly reveal how these behaviors extended beyond the meetings of the Parlay House to the general population. Our aim was to design a survey that could tell us more about the various forms that the Parlay Effect takes, as well as the thoughts and feelings people have experienced when they have been a part of a Parlay Effect cascade.

Our process involved designing and administering an online survey using TurkPrime, a platform that allows behavioral researchers to recruit participants worldwide. We collected data from 344 participants in the United States ranging in age from 18 to 40 years old, with a fairly equal balance of men and women.

Participants completed one of three possible versions of the survey, determined randomly. Each version inquired about their prior participation in a Parlay Effect cascade, but the three versions differed based on whether they were referring to a time when they took action to initiate a cascade, whether they were the recipient of a Parlay Effect action, or whether they were witness to a Parlay Effect cascade that involved other people.

In other words, participants in the first group framed their responses to our questions in the role of the Initiator in the Parlay Effect: the person who does something empathetic, kind, generous or thoughtful for someone else without any expectation of return, which then leads to a cascade of some kind.

Participants in the second group responded as the Recipient of such an action: someone who is the recipient of some form of thoughtfulness and is then moved to extend that positive gesture to yet another person.

The final participant group served as the Witness to an act underlying the Parlay Effect.

Our goal for the third group was to investigate the different kinds of actions that could lead to a Parlay Effect, the reasons why people engage in an action that leads to the Parlay Effect and the feelings people experience when initiating, receiving or bearing witness to a Parlay Effect cascade.

The results were fascinating, and you'll read about them in Anne's introduction and throughout the book, in the inspiring personal stories that she tells.

In working with Anne on this research study, I was not only inspired by all that she has learned, accomplished and supported through her efforts and activities, but also reminded of the fundamentally good, kind and generous nature of most people.

The Parlay Effect happens more than most people would probably think. Cascades that are at the core of the Parlay Effect can occur in multiple ways—it's not just about money or connections. The Parlay Effect is not reserved for people who have the luxury to initiate such an action. Anyone can start a cascade, without much time, effort or resources. It does, however, take some awareness and an inclination to appreciate that small actions on one's own part can ripple outward, leading to positive consequences beyond oneself. The effect makes people feel good in all sorts of psychologically beneficial ways that are both good for individuals and good for society.

The Parlay Effect is fundamentally timeless and universal. It is not restricted to a specific time, country or set of people. It's always worth reminding people about the potential power and good that it can set in motion. It's also the case, though, that the current state of the world, and of our country in particular, makes reminders about the good that we can do for others through the Parlay Effect particularly valuable. Whether the Parlay Effect is put to use at the level of one's own community, with a stranger, or with one's friends, family or neighbors—it's relevant and has the power to make positive change.

STARTING A NEW CHAPTER

In the long run, we shape our lives, and we shape ourselves. The process never ends, until we die. And the choices we make are ultimately our own responsibility.

— ELEANOR ROOSEVELT

NEARLY 50 YEARS AFTER COMING INTO THIS WORLD, I began my life for a second time. I had been CEO at several different advertising agencies in New York City and was a single mother of two daughters. I considered myself an energetic, healthy and vibrant woman with a bright future. Then, in one year, I lost almost every piece of myself. During the 2010 recession, I was diagnosed with recurring cancer and was ignominiously replaced in my job because of it. To top it off, my youngest daughter left for college, so that I was on my own again. It was a trifecta of setbacks. I lost all context, grounding and perspective.

Until that point, I had introduced myself as, "I'm the CEO." Or, "I'm Lauren and Ciara's mom." Or "Yep. I'm the one who loves getting to the gym at 5 a.m. before work." Without these ways to frame myself, I didn't know who I was or where my life was going.

What's more, most of the relationships I had built while running companies and raising my children proved to be more mirage than reality. Although I had worked with thousands of people over my career and knew many people in my community, when I became sick and lost my position of power, most of them disappeared. I could count on one hand the number of people who were there for me—a couple of girlfriends and family members. It was David—my long-distance boyfriend of a few years, who really showed up. He was with me through the surgery and then cheered me on afterward, encouraging me to walk a few blocks into Central Park two days after I left the hospital to see Shakespeare in the Park—with Al Pacino in *The Merchant of Venice*—just to prove to myself that I was still alive and that I had more life yet to come.

But exactly what life would that be? Who was I, without a big career, without children at home who gave me a sense of purpose, and without a community where I felt connected? I floundered. I was un-tethered, overwhelmed, isolated. I slipped from a place of confidence, routine and familiarity into an emotional and physical free fall.

David suggested that I move out to California, to be with him in Santa Cruz. I'm a city girl, and the jump between Manhattan and Santa Cruz seemed too great for me. So we negotiated and settled on San Francisco as a place where we could build a life together. Brought up in Seattle, I was familiar with the West Coast. Yet San Francisco was a new city to me—a beautiful one, filled with new opportunities and many possibilities for a chance at a restart, but a city where I knew no one.

When I moved to San Francisco, I had no plans and no friends. I knew only David, who was absorbed by his skyrocketing career, an esteemed teaching position, children at home who still needed him, and an intense dedication to social justice initiatives. By contrast, I had no routine and no direction. I was passionate about everything and nothing, it seemed. And while I was fortunate to have a partner who could support me, not pulling my own financial weight made me feel like a failure. Looking back, I don't remember ever feeling that badly about myself or that alone, even while surrounded by the beauty of the Bay Area and the love of my life.

I forced myself to craft a new chapter of my life. I was still struggling to know just what to do, and at the same time, I realized that it was a rare luxury to have a choice about how to create a new life. I spent a lot of time alone with my emotions and insecurities, and I tried to balance those feelings with concrete ideas about what my future might hold. Should I run another company? Start a nonprofit? Pursue my love of clothing and jewelry design? There was no clear answer, but eventually, a path forward started to form.

For the past 25 years, I had slugged it out as a female CEO in the very male world of advertising. It was arguably a successful period for me, in terms of rising up the corporate ladder, but it also left me isolated and lacking a sense of real connection with the people who worked with me.

In fact, it was exactly that sense of connection that I craved as I looked ahead. I longed to recapture the emotional richness of experiences in my past: the intense and fulfilling years I had spent at Wellesley College, my close relationships with my two sisters, and the dramatic and wonderful "house of hormones" where I had raised my daughters. I came to realize that, despite my accomplishments as a leader and executive, these were the highlights of my life.

I wanted new interactions that were deep and meaningful, and which flowed from a true sense of giving rather than from the quid pro quos that are too often the basis of professional life.

Never a "lady who lunches," I knew that traditional social clubs weren't the answer for me. Such clubs were communities of "selective inclusion," and although I was welcomed because of my pedigree, I realized that those who didn't have those advantages would not be, and this troubled me. It also did not solve my craving for meeting people who broadened my own experience, in part because they were not just like me. I was seeking something both familiar and entirely new.

The first taste of the type of organization I wanted to build came in 2003. After I was chosen to be a Henry Crown Fellow of the Aspen Institute in Colorado, I spent two years meeting regularly with 20 "classmates" to read the classics, poetry and contemporary essays, and to discuss how they applied to our lives as leaders and our quest to "live the good life." The combination of this content, which gave us all a common focus, with a safe environment where we could talk openly about how the ideas related to us personally, was a revelation. It underscored that the "good life" was not about accumulating wealth, but about doing good and feeling good. It was a magical, transformative time—and a major clue as to how I could create something meaningful going forward.

As it turns out, the Aspen Institute had deliberately created a forum where people who were not alike in superficial terms (of age, race, sexual orientation, political views or career track) could find commonalities and a platform to support each other. This was inherently what I wanted to emulate, in some new way.

Dr. Katherine Phillips, professor of leadership and ethics management at Columbia Business School, has done a lot of research on the benefits of diversity. It turns out that in a myriad of settings (whether in personal relationships, in academic study, or business and social situations), partners who have complementary but different strategies actually enjoy more positive relationships. Lisa Tiedens, president of Scripps College, has also worked on this subject, and concurs that partnerships/relationships/work teams are more productive when people pair with others who are different from them. Arthur Aaron, currently a visiting professor at the University of California, Berkeley, concludes that dissimilarity enhances attraction, because it increases the potential for "self-expansion." The greater the difference between you and the person or people you pair with, the greater is the opportunity for new perspectives that can enrich you.

I set out to replicate that magic of growth through difference— and to do it by building a community of women. Ideally, the organization I envisioned would include a wide-ranging group of dynamic women and provide a safe place for us to gather, laugh, relax, talk about important ideas and, for at least a few hours every month, put ourselves first, something women rarely do. I wanted to explore this idea of self-expansion.

I took a leap of faith and jumped in, inviting a few women—friends of friends, Aspen Institute alumnae and people I'd met at the dog park—to come to my home. Only about a dozen showed up at the first get-together, and they were not people I knew well. Most I didn't know at all. What I also didn't know was that this gathering of women at my house once a month would become a vibrant organization. I just wanted to create a safe and nurturing space for the people who often relegated themselves to the bottom of the "care hierarchy," putting family members, jobs and community activities ahead of self-care. So I offered champagne and snacks as well as content that stimulated conversation and provided much-needed nurturing and attention.

The initial gatherings of 20 or so women became something that many of us looked forward to every month. They offered us an opportunity to put ourselves first and make satisfying connections. We named our organization "Parlay House" because we realized these gatherings had the power to help others parlay one chapter of life into another, and to use our strengths to help one another. "Parlay" also conveniently sounds like the French word *parler*, which means "to speak," which I translated as helping women to find their voices. It also, in the world of gambling, means "to wager winnings on a subsequent event:" simply, *to place a small bet on a bigger outcome*. I instinctively knew that my bet on the Parlay House, to connect women with other women, would translate into bigger things. What I didn't know at first is how it would all play out.

At one of our first events, Tamsin Smith, a friend and poet, moved us by reading her work and the work of other poets. At another gathering, Shabana Basij-Rasikh, a young Afghan woman who, during the regime of the Taliban, had dressed as a boy to escort her burqa-clad sister to an underground school, talked about how her experience inspired her to create a school for girls in Afghanistan. One of the most emotionally charged events was a candid account by Katie Hafner, a *New York Times* journalist and best-selling author, of how her alcoholic mother, from whom she had been separated as a child, moved in with her and her teenage daughter decades later.

As the content became more intimate and compelling, we found common insights, and we realized that it was time to talk about the group's values. We agreed that Parlay House would be a new form of community where women of different ages, races, experience, income and interests could gather in a safe and welcoming environment. We wanted our group to be opt-in, where people attended events based on whether they were interested in the topic that month and because they identified with the idea of women supporting other women. And we wanted our community to represent a sort of inclusive diversity that was missing for us in the separate bubbles of our personal lives.

In those early days, we made two rules, which haven't changed:

1.   Each new member would be brought in, and be taken care of, by an existing member, so she would not feel alone.

2.   The gatherings would never be used for professional or monetary gain. Even though networking for the sake of career advancement may happen naturally, we all agreed that pursuing it explicitly would detract from the intimacy of our time together and should be taken up outside our meetings.

That's it.

With these rules in place, the group flourished. We talked about what was missing from our lives. Many felt alone, as I had, lacking meaningful and trusting connection with other women. Others in the group were at transitional stages in their lives, without a clear direction on how to move forward. A few people wanted to contribute more to their communities around them but didn't know how. And almost all agreed that despite our accomplishments, we felt as if our own happiness often ended up as the last priority—the bottom of the social hierarchy amid our obligations to our families, work and relationships. We put everyone else around us first. In joining the group, we had the comfort of knowing that an entire cadre of women was operating on the same plane, feeling the things we were feeling.

In no time, Parlay House gatherings were sold out, and membership—simply thanks to individual women inviting a friend or an acquaintance to the gatherings—exploded. Month after month, the organization blossomed, as members pulled more people into our inclusive circle. The original handful of women soon grew to a group of 300, then 600, and now thousands across the country and Europe. With this validation and enthusiasm, I saw what Parlay House really is: an inclusive community where the events help people who are at inflection points and crossroads find connection and strength. I also saw that the gatherings actually trigger a series of micro-actions that extend far beyond our group. One woman finds herself in a position to help another through kindness, empathy, generosity or encouragement, and the woman who received that help then replicates it, passing it on to another woman.

I call this "one small thing,"™ which often reflects the strengths of each woman and which cascades into a series of positive experiences, the "Parlay Effect." For most of us, this phrase conjures up the image of the *domino effect,* the cumulative effect produced when one event sets off a chain of similar events. We've been conditioned to see in our minds that when dominoes are set in motion, they fall. The Parlay Effect, in contrast, conjures up just the opposite. When women are set in motion, they lift each other up, rather than push each other down. Empowered by other women, women don't just pay it forward; they pay it outward.

What distinguishes women's strengths from men's is an interesting question. According to Gallup's widely used Clifton Strengths-Finder, women and men share four of the five top strengths—Learner, Responsibility, Relator and Input. For the fifth strength, the finding differs.

Men round out as Achievers, whereas women round out with Empathy. In my view, this distinction can be used effectively to create meaningful change. Empathy involves a close awareness of others and some sense of intimacy, while achievement is about relative success. Gallup's findings suggest that, compared to men, women are generally more inclined to focus on groups or teams and gather collective voices. Women tend to be more sensitive and intuitive about what is going on with the people around them. Men, on the other hand, are more prone to gather external data and internalize their decision-making. Rather than asking for feedback from others, men tend to look for answers from within.

It is important to note that these discoveries apply to men and women in general and do not apply to individual men and women. Differences are much greater *within* genders than between genders. The takeaway, though, is that if women are set up to empathize—to include and to encourage others—the Parlay Effect has enormous innate potential.

PROVING IT

I wondered how big that potential could be and whether the chain of inclusion is linear. As one woman brings another, and she the next, are these acts of inclusion somehow larger and magnifying?

Throughout this book, I have drawn on research from social scientists who helped explain and flesh out key concepts. None of the existing research, however, could track with specificity the outcomes I observed with the Parlay Effect.

As you read in Dr. Serena Chen's Foreword, we decided to work together to conduct a new and proprietary study, because we wanted to better understand how the behaviors associated with the Parlay Effect carried over from the Parlay House and on out to the general population. The examples of a Parlay Effect suggested in the survey were wide-ranging:

- giving food to a homeless person and seeing them share it with others;
- teaching colleagues or friends a skill that they could then use to help someone else;
- passing children's clothing to a mom with younger children and then seeing her share with another mom;
- including a stranger in an event and then seeing this person invite other new people into their circle.

The results were fascinating.

Our research discovered cultural familiarity with the concept of "paying it forward." A significant number of respondents in all three categories (Initiator, Recipient and Witness) had heard of the concept and demonstrated it by buying a coffee or food for the person behind them in line. They could often report the number of people in their chain reaction, because they went back to the establishment or watched it unfold. While I was skeptical of their actions—thinking that they were repeating a story they had heard about, rather than having a genuine feeling of connection to a stranger—I discovered that I was wrong in that assumption. Initiating or participating in a chain of buying something for the next person was certainly part of a positive cascade, but it provided a surprising sense of community for those involved. Whether manufactured, formalized or initiating from the person, it all had the meaningful effect of making participants feel part of something bigger—belonging to this community of strangers, even if it was a short-lived connection.

Surprisingly, our research also measured an effect *beyond* "paying it forward."

In all three of our research groups, respondents reported instances of "passing material resources on to someone else in need" more frequently than any other kind of generous act. In some examples, it was a small but helpful sum of money that allowed the recipients to feed their families. For others, it was the passing on of items to someone else whose need seemed greater than their own. Many of these examples began with one person noticing and internalizing someone else's predicament and finding a way to help.

The second most frequently mentioned action by all three groups was also related to giving—but the giving of one's time rather than the giving of material goods. Much of this generosity came in the form of coaching, teaching and encouraging. And again, most of the actions were sparked by the initiator's awareness of someone else's need and the desire to reduce their burden. Empathy strikes again.

In general, Initiators of the Parlay Effect were the most empathetic: seeing someone in need and figuring out an easy and small way to help them. The most common positive actions were not intended to make huge social change, cost large sums of money or take lots of time. In fact, many of the meaningful actions consisted of simple gestures that most people have the time and resources for, such as helping someone short on cash to buy a few groceries, or seeing someone going through a hard time and reaching out to offer comfort and support. This is encouraging in that it means that most, if not all, of us can find ways to begin or continue a Parlay Effect, no matter what our income or life situation.

People who were the beneficiaries (Recipients) of a helpful/kind/generous act tended to try to replicate a comparable act themselves. If they received some sort of financial assistance, they passed on financial support to someone else. If someone offered them mentoring or coaching, they tried to coach another person. If someone made them feel "seen" or included, they chose to see and include others. A clear implication of these results is that if we want to see specific changes in our world, acting in the way we hope that others might act can start a cascade of change. Our research validates Gandhi's maxim "Be the change you wish to see in the world."

Recipients of encouragement and advice (as well as Witnesses of supportive actions) seemed to feel empowered as a result of having been encouraged, and then chose to pass on this encouragement or coaching to another person.

THE KICKER

Beyond the heartwarming process of tracking positive acts from person to person, the most significant and surprising result of the research came neither from the giver, nor from the recipient. Witnesses (people who were solely observers of a kind/generous/ helpful action, rather than the instigators or the recipients) actually took on the task of initiating and creating a new chain themselves! After seeing someone else give or benefit, the Witnesses became increasingly motivated to behave in these positive ways themselves. A significant number of them chose to take positive action as a result of seeing another person's initiative.

The big finding from our study is that our Parlay Effect is not just one-to-one, but is multiplied exponentially, as people observe positive acts and begin to pass them on. At a time when many of us feel that our ability to effect meaningful change is limited and that we don't know where to start, realizing that an action from one person to another can be amplified and replicated at an exponential level generates hope that small actions can truly be part of a significant cascade of good.

While I had expected that participation in a social group like a church, a charity or a cause would trigger the greatest number of Parlay Effects, the majority of the positive activities we tracked turned out to have been initiated and perpetuated by individuals and were not generated by a group. Moreover, they did not originate from rules or obligations set by any group. The people who reported initiating or passing along positive actions did so based on personal choice and social values. This opens up the possibility for many disenfranchised individuals to experience an increased sense of control over both their own lives and the lives of others, without having to depend on group-think or prescriptive activities. It speaks to the ability we each have to be agents of change in things that matter to us personally.

Recipients of kind acts did not suspect the motivation of the givers. We had feared that recipients would feel that the givers were being kind or generous in the hope of some sort of personal gain, or simply because it made them feel good, but the research showed very little evidence of this. The assumption that Parlay Effect actions| are self-serving or transactional in nature was not borne out by the findings.

This is not to say that the Parlay Effect didn't have an emotional impact—quite the contrary. Participants connected many positive emotions with what they had witnessed, and most of these held true whether they were involved as an Initiator, Recipient or Witness. The most commonly mentioned results of the Parlay Effect were joy, inspiration, energy, peace, confidence, clarity, pride, inclusion, connection, belonging, empowerment and strength. How many other situations can you think of that are attainable for everyone and generate such rich emotional outcomes?

Interestingly, the Parlay Effect elicited almost no negative emotions. The only negative emotion that scored at all was a sense of obligation, a feeling that not participating and failing to pay it forward might result in feelings of shame. Such feelings are understandable, and can probably be attributed to the sense that one is responsible to society.

At a time in history when many people feel that our country and our world fall short in terms of leadership, disparities in wealth, and a lack of acceptance and inclusion, this research offers proof that it really is possible to take small actions that have a significant impact.

———

My hope in writing this book is to show how easy it is to begin with a very small action, One Small Thing™, which springs from a personal strength that can have a much greater impact than the giver could have imagined. It's the good that happens as a result of something else good. It's the "thing after the thing."

In this book, I'll take you on my journey of personal transformation and share what I have observed about the paths of personal development that others have taken. Each is unique, and yet the journeys have much in common. I will give you specific guidelines, tools and insight from our research about how to use those inflection points in life to launch cascades of change for you and those around you—to show you how you, too, can be part of the Parlay Effect.

With this book, it is my privilege to help women empower other women. When this happens, the effect is exponential, and we all rise. We are stronger when we are connected.

CHAPTER 01

START WITH
THE SPACE
IN BETWEEN

And the trouble is, if you don't risk anything, you risk more.

— ERICA JONG

IN OUR RESEARCH, WE SAW THAT THE PARLAY EFFECT often began with observing another person, whether struggling, lost or hungry. In my own case, it was when I started hearing phrases uttered by other women that resonated with me at a soul-level. I heard them talk about feeling embarrassed about being in-between jobs. It was the admission by another woman that she was hypercritical of her body or hearing the desperation in someone's voice that she would never find a satisfying personal relationship. Listening to people who were struggling with some of the issues I was struggling with, and having them say it out loud, made me feel less alone and set me out on a quest to reground myself.

It was through that experience that I found the inspiration to start Parlay House and study its effects. I was at a personal inflection point—a point of transition—from a life that was defined by what I did for a living, to a life for which I had not yet found a focus. It was when I stopped to look inside myself, to be less hard on myself and to think about the changes that would make a difference for me, that I began to see a solution.

I am hard-pressed to think of anyone in my life who has avoided a major personal crossroads, whether an illness, a divorce, a professional challenge, financial difficulties or concern over a parent or child. The truth is that life presents a set of challenges to all of us. What I came to realize over time was that plowing through my challenges—conquering them through sheer determination, strength and rational problem-solving—was not always the best solution.

Finding a way to live comfortably in the space that follows a setback in your life and before finding your new direction is crucial. It is a way of taking stock and a way to look both inward and outward before committing to the next chapter in your life. At the same time, it is also important not to get stuck in the transitional period. Navigating between one phase and another is easier said than done, but you can learn certain ways to help you keep afloat.

My time in "the space in between" was not a conscious choice. I was visiting the Kabalagala Community Academy in Uganda, a primary school for disadvantaged and orphaned children that I had helped to build a few years earlier, when I received an unexpected call from my oncologist. For 10 years, this physician had been my partner as I battled cervical cancer, and I had seen him the week before I left, for our usual test: snip and wait. Usually, it was the nurse who called with the results. This time, the doctor called himself.

Through the crackly connection on the line to Africa, I tried to mentally process what he was saying: The hysterectomy I had undergone years before had not been able to stop my cancer from spreading. In fact, its progress had accelerated, and we could no longer manage it by waiting and watching. I needed major surgery.

I remember noticing that, as he spoke, I felt a sharp pain in my heart, as if I was being stabbed. There had been few times in my life that I had experienced emotional pain as physical pain, but this time it was unmistakable. I was afraid. Panic-stricken. My mind raced. What if I died? What if I was unable to care for my children? After the call, as tears welled up, I channeled the comforting words that my partner, David, or my closest friends would have shared. I heard my sister Rachel's voice loudly in my head: "Take a deep breath. Now another."

It was a true low point in my life. Yet, surrounded by Kabalagala's poverty and despair, sifting through the hardship around me to find the nuggets of joy in our makeshift school, I had no choice but to put my own concerns into a "mental coping box" and shut the lid. Processing would have to come later. I didn't want to worry my eldest daughter, Lauren, who was teaching at the school for the summer, or to abandon the students I'd come to see. They had been left behind so many times before, as had my daughter, in her own way. When I divorced her father, she, too, had lost a parent.

For the rest of my visit, I focused on the remarkably resilient children, most of whom found happiness at school despite their own dire circumstances. I saw that they shared difficult truths, about their dead parents, and what they knew of poverty, abuse and neglect. The joy of learning and the community they experienced with each other made them feel safe, and less alone. These lessons leapt out from my experiences in Uganda and stayed with me in the weeks and months to come.

Back home, I set out to do what I had always done: deal with the obstacle in front of me, and try to continue on regardless. I wouldn't let a health setback get in the way of my career. I would take a few weeks off, have the surgery and jump right back into the fray. I already knew how to build and lead advertising agencies. I would just do that again.

LET GO AND LOOK WITHIN

Mentoring other women, I often talk about being aware of patterns of linear thinking; the false assumption that the door to success or happiness lies just ahead. When we think in a linear way, we assume that we are on the "right" path and doing the "right" things; we just need to do more of the same. We believe we can break through to success and happiness if we just push harder, work longer and steel ourselves against vulnerability.

Think about it. We climb up the corporate ladder. We try to break through the glass ceiling. We assume that a chronology of events will unfold, from graduation to career to relationships to children to success and then retirement. But while we are looking ahead and hoping to move up, more often than not, we miss all that is around us. We are blind to our other strengths and our alternatives, because we are looking ahead of ourselves instead of within and around ourselves.

Eckhart Tolle, best known as the author of *The Power of Now* and *A New Earth* and named one of the most spiritually influential people in the world by Watkins Review, has written many books on consciousness. He observes that "Nothing ever happened in the past; it happened in the now. Nothing will ever happen in the future; it will happen in the now." As Tolle sees it, plowing ahead on the premise that the past will drive the future is a failure to realize and take advantage of the power of the present, and of the fact that we can only take action in a given moment. If we act aggressively, thinking only of what has worked in the past or of our hopes for the future, and if we do not take time to reflect on the present, we reduce our awareness of both internal and external needs and opportunities.

Some people realize at a very young age that the "road less traveled" is for them, but most people do not have this clarity of direction. Typically, we need to practice trying new things before we can realize that pushing ahead harder, faster and stronger doesn't always yield the results we want. It often takes a series of minor, iterative shifts to help us embrace more of the things we do well, and that we love to do, and to move away from the areas that do not feel meaningful or natural. But the deeper we get into a career, a relationship, a project or a lifestyle, the harder it is to let go. The faster we are going, the more likely it is that we will miss opportunities to see whether other more satisfying paths are open for us.

The crossroads or inflection points in life often present themselves as markers such as birthdays and promotions. They often include a change in relationship status (good or bad), a disappointing failure or a rejection in your career, or the illness or even death of a friend or family member. Whatever the cause, the trick is to pay attention to our feelings and what they call on us to do, rather than what we think we are supposed to do. Our feelings can signal to us whether we are too far removed from our natural strengths and interests, or a situation that causes more stress and pain than joy and ease. As Tolle would say, we need to be conscious about being in the present, because that state of awareness will lead us to greater clarity.

CANCER, JOB LOSS AND AN EMPTY NEST

In 2010, at the low point of the financial recession, my company was in turnaround and I was not in my sweet spot. I was far from the energetic start-up specialty units that I was used to creating. Morale was low, and I had to execute a number of very painful downsizings. I was giving it my all, refusing to fail, pushing as hard as I could each day to encourage our organization, pitch new business, retain existing clients whose budgets were shrinking along with their revenues, and do strong creative work in an increasingly risk-averse environment. On my flight back to New York from Uganda, I decided I would take a brief hiatus, have the surgery and return as quickly as I could afterward to maintain the company's momentum.

A few weeks before the scheduled surgery, I confidently walked into my corporate headquarters wearing my usual 4-inch heels and projecting confidence. I was eager to confirm my plan with my boss. I instantly realized, however, that something was off. He entered our meeting quietly, with his head down. There was none of our usual banter—updates on the kids, overviews of the new business pipeline. And, worst of all, no eye contact.

He was brief: "Don't hate me for this, but we're going to have someone else run the company." Period. He didn't say, "The job will be here for you until you get well" or "I want you to have time to heal" or even "You have done an amazing job for us." He essentially said, "You are fired."

I was stunned. Until that moment, my priorities in life were:

1. Motherhood
2. My career
3. David, the love of my life
4. The kids in Uganda

The rest of the list (being a good daughter, sister, friend, community participant, athlete) took a back seat. Way back.

It all came in a flood. My younger daughter, Ciara, was preparing to start college at Tulane University in New Orleans. My elder daughter, Lauren, was returning to school in Los Angeles. My health was at risk and I was their only parent. The challenges in Uganda seemed insurmountable. And now my job was yanked away from me by a person I had completely trusted. I had moved from New York City, where I felt at home, to the New Jersey suburbs where, as a single mother holding a big, full-time job, I felt like an outsider, alienated from the moms and families. My entire world was upside down.

David, who lived in Santa Cruz, California, flew across the country to be by my side for the operation. One of the many shocks I faced while healing was realizing how few friends I really had. Apart from David and my immediate family, I could count on one hand the number of people who reached out to me. I will forever hold tightly my memories of the few who visited, proving that we had a connection beyond the workplace. But I never heard from the vast majority of people with whom I had worked for decades, and that was devastating for me. I could no longer do anything for them or their careers, and as a result, I was no longer relevant to them. While I was deeply saddened by that experience, it was also an important lesson in how I would live the next phase of my life.

I could have done what I had done so many times before: find a new job running another agency. Make lemonade out of lemons. Plow ahead. And if David had not been in the picture, that is probably what I would have done, and fallen into the potentially fatal error of looking only straight ahead in my quest for fulfillment. But with David, I had found not only true love, but also the first real sense that I didn't have to fight my battles alone. I began to understand the importance of trusting relationships and supportive communities, and to becoming more open to paths I'd never thought to explore.

For over 20 years, I had been my own partner. Now I had someone to catch me if I fell, someone with whom I could share my fears and vulnerabilities. I also had someone who was very open to taking unconventional paths, someone who encouraged me to stop and think about what I wanted next. There was no reason that I had to go back into advertising. No reason why I had to stay in New York while David remained in California. The "musts" I had lived were replaced by "what ifs."

PAY ATTENTION TO THE KNOCK AT THE SIDE DOOR

I am certainly not the only person who has had to learn the hard lesson that pausing to reflect is wiser than plowing ahead. Those of us who have had to make major changes later in life cannot help but reach back to strategies and approaches that have worked in the past. Sometimes, tried and true processes provide an easy fix, but doing the same thing over and over can lead just as quickly to stagnation rather than growth.

RACHEL: INSPIRATION FROM AN UNEXPECTED SOURCE

My sister Rachel has been making hand-designed stationery since the day she graduated from Colby College more than 30 years ago. Since she left college, she has always been self-employed, designing invitations, cards, logos and many forms of beautifully crafted materials for her own small business. As you might expect, managing a small business in times of economic stress and evolving technology is a challenge. While she was able to develop and maintain a wide-ranging and impressive client base, keeping profitable has been exceptionally hard work. But she made her way for three decades, step after step, in the direction that she had charted for herself.

Rachel's company had finally reached a level where it could sustain itself. Big-time clients were reaching out with more requests and larger orders than she had ever received. But at the moment when the quality of her work and the effectiveness of her service were finally being validated, she wasn't celebrating. Instead, just when she would have expected to feel joy and accomplishment, she realized that she was miserable. She wasn't thrilled to get the calls and orders; instead, she felt creatively stuck and burned out. Rachel describes it as feeling that she had a hole inside her that made her feel empty.

Day after day, and week after week, she soldiered on, hoping to regain her passion, her creative edge. But the emptiness grew, and not a day went by that she did not feel consumed by the loss of some part of herself.

Rachel didn't wake up one morning with clarity about how to address this crossroads. Instead, she started to pay attention to other parts of her life, where new ideas and new sources of inspiration were emerging. She could find nothing of interest at a New York stationery trade show, and yet she couldn't stop thinking about a food-truck rodeo that she had visited in Brooklyn. The food trucks drew her not only because the food they offered was so diverse but also because of the personal stories the vendors could tell.

Returning to Seattle, it hit her, in a proverbial "Eureka!" moment, as she walked through Pioneer Square. Why not create her own version of a food-truck experience, using her original craft of hand-written letters and stationery? In 2016, she launched the Letter Farmer, a mobile pop-up letter-writing experience packed into a Sprinter van filled with cards, stationery and stamps. Every day, she pulls up to an approved location in Seattle, opens her doors, unfolds café tables, and sets up places where people can come and write. Putting pen to paper, and jettisoning the all-purpose text abbreviations like LMK and LMAO, her customers thoughtfully reach out with heartfelt words and phrases like "I miss our time together" or "I am so grateful for the lessons you taught me."

While many Letter Farmer patrons are working people intrigued by the reintroduction of letter writing and the beauty of her cards, Rachel has found that some of the most inspired users of her services are the homeless and disenfranchised in her community. Many have long lost touch with family and friends as they wander the streets, fight addiction or battle mental illness. She sees that by giving them inspirational ideas to get started, and providing free pens, paper, envelopes and stamps, they are happy to sit and write.

As a result, through cards and letters, parents are hearing from their children, even if it is only a simple confirmation that they are still alive. Meanwhile, friends are reconnecting with friends and the lucky recipients are thrilled to find something in the mail that is not a bill.

Rachel doesn't read the personal notes but instead, facilitates that action of writing and connecting with loved ones. The letters written at the café tables outside the Letter Farmer van have reached across the globe and begun meaningful conversations that will unfold in ways we can only imagine.

If Rachel had not taken the time to stop and reassess her path, it's likely she would have blindly forged ahead, losing that sense of passion and mission. The door to the next phase in her life was not in front of her. Instead, it was off to the side, inspired by a chance experience and closely bound up with something that was important to her. Combining a new experience and an old passion resulted in something she could pass along to others, creating a cascade of reconnection and providing a voice to those who had lost their own.

WHEN THE OPEN DOOR IS NOT STRAIGHT AHEAD

Both for Rachel and for me, the open door was neither directly in front of us nor behind us. It was located at a pause point, a crossroads that drew upon our experiences from the past while we stopped to assess our lives. Instead of replicating former goals, the pause allowed us to revisit our values and envision a new way forward.

But for other people, the path is not immediately visible. It can take years before our choices show that our actions and values are complementary.

THE PLACE OF DEEP UNKNOWING

We live in a fast-paced society where it is unsettling to move on from all that is familiar to us. The experience leaves us vulnerable. What if our world moves on without us while we are stopping to reassess? How will our new choices affect the lives of people we love? I worried how my children would be affected when I moved to San Francisco from New Jersey. Perhaps most scary of all, what would happen if I took the plunge and failed to find new ideas or inspiration?

Being at a crossroads can be frightening, but I believe that we all have moments in our lives, at points of transition, where we need to fight the urge to keep going without thinking, and to reach only for safety. William Stafford, an American writer known for his approachable, articulate poems, makes the point beautifully in "A Ritual to Read to Each Other:"

> If you don't know the kind of person I am
> and I don't know the kind of person you are
> a pattern that others made may prevail in the world
> and following the wrong god home we may miss our star.

This speaks to the importance of knowing yourself and allowing that self-awareness to inform your choices about how you live your life. Stafford describes it as "missing our star." Too often, we are following an assumed truth of how things should be—a "truth" that was set by others and does not necessarily ring true for us now, or maybe ever.

Our crossroads is a place of deep unknowing. Sometimes the consequences of a choice can seem so monumental that we act quickly, just to get the decision over with. The challenge is to do the opposite, to wait until clarity comes. Thomas Moore summed it up well in his best-selling book *Care of the Soul*:

> How many times do we lose an occasion for soul work by leaping ahead to final solutions without pausing to savor the undertones? We are a radically bottom-line society, eager to act and to end tension, and thus we lose opportunities to know ourselves for our motives and our secrets.

For me, that clarity came when I realized the extent of my imperfections: I saw that I couldn't be the Superwoman of my past...or maybe that I had never been Superwoman at all.

START WITH A ROLE MODEL

When you're at an inflection point, finding or becoming a role model can often help you start to make a change. Social psychology has found significant evidence that role models can not only invoke inspiration, but also help people view themselves more positively and increase their motivation. Such "self-enhancement" can happen if the role models are in walks of life relevant to the recipient; for example, a scientist would not be an effective role model for an aspiring soccer player, but a professional tennis player might be. The role model must be accessible and relevant to produce positive effects.

JULIE: THE LONG REACH OF THE ROLE MODEL

Julie Abrams, a 26-year-old graduate student with a newborn baby, stood out in the immigrant community where she lived in Little

Village, Chicago. She had a strong sense of herself, and prided herself as a problem solver; when people called her "strong and bossy," she happily owned it.

One morning, while Julie was holding a newborn baby in one arm and textbooks in the other, her telephone rang. At the other end of the line was Carmina, a 13-year-old neighbor and recent immigrant from Mexico, who had been attacked by a group of boys while walking the two blocks to her school. As she tried to recover from the attack, the only person Carmina could think to call was Julie, the rare strong and courageous woman on her block. Carmina told Julie that she felt afraid and alone and had decided it was too dangerous to go back to school.

Even at 26, Julie was willing to take action. When Carmina talked about quitting school because she didn't feel safe anymore, Julie stepped up. She persuaded Carmina's mother to let Julie become her temporary legal guardian, to help her navigate school and homework and to provide her a loving family environment. Carmina's mother, who did not have the benefit of an education or a strong grasp of the English language, seemed relieved to have Julie take her daughter under her wing. Carmina was welcomed wholeheartedly into the Abrams family, joining them at Marquette Park, at family gatherings and on holidays. While Carmina was quiet, she was a keen observer of her surroundings; she settled in comfortably to the very different cadence of her temporary home. She watched Julie love, raise and nurture her children, and she too received that love and nurturing.

But the love and nurturing also came with rules—about doing homework, about safety and about responsibility. When Carmina turned 15 and was allowed to make her own choices about where she would live, she chose to move back in with her mother, where she did not have the structure or support that she'd grown accustomed to under Julie's care. Julie had believed that Carmina would choose to pursue her education, build strong family values, and have a chance to break out of the cycle of poverty that plagued her family of origin. But away from Julie's protective watch, Carmina soon found herself single and pregnant, not once but twice. She and Julie lost touch, leaving Julie with the sense that the guidance she had tried to provide for her had come to nothing.

More than 15 years later, Julie received an unexpected message from Carmina on Facebook. Carmina was reaching out because she was now the mother of teenagers who were about to reach a higher level of education than she had achieved herself. Carmina had come to realize, more than a decade later, that Julie had been a role model for her, encouraging her to raise her children in a way that prepared them for successful adult lives. Slowly, message after message and call after call, Julie has resumed her position in Carmina's life as mentor, coach and now friend. It took time for Julie's kindness to influence and empower Carmina, enough to change her path and that of her children, who will soon be the first in their family to graduate from high school.

It turns out that Julie had not only taken Carmina in as a child but had remained a role model for her in a way that kept communications open. My sister Rachel, on the other hand, did not have a clear role model for revitalizing her career, but used her natural creative thinking as she faced her own inflection point, letting herself be guided by inspiration from an unexpected place. In my own case, I reached inside myself to evaluate my personal history, to feel what was missing and to test out potential solutions.

Whether you find an increased sense of clarity about the next step from another person, a new experience or a new emotion, you must leave yourself open to a constant process of reassessment and growth: the shedding of the old to make room for the new.

QUESTIONS TO ASK, STEPS TO TAKE:

How do you embark on an assessment of your path and yourself? What if you feel you are not at a point in your life where you can make significant change?

My feeling is that the sooner you get to know yourself, the more open you will be to the subtle signals that change can give you new energy, interest and momentum. In fact, it's great to practice knowing yourself by taking small steps now, so that when you reach a roadblock or crisis, looking inward is not so daunting.

GETTING TO KNOW YOURSELF EXERCISE

Recall an experience from your past that occurred long enough ago to give you the distance to analyze it as an outside observer. Use a memory from an early relationship, from your first years at work or from an experience that particularly arouses your emotions. Think of the situation and ask yourself these questions:

* Why does this event stand out for me, and what does it tell me about my reaction to a disappointment, a challenge or a threat?

* Did I tackle it alone, or did I gather allies around me?

- What did the pain feel like? (Where did you feel it in your body?)

- If your response was to push forward right away, would you say this approach was successful? Or, looking back, would it have been better to act more slowly?

- Most people find it difficult to revisit that "pocket of pain," even though it can be very instructive for us to do so. If you were able to stay with the pain, can you remember how you managed to do that? Have you used that skill again in life since then?

- What was your reaction? Some people may feel immediately defensive. Others might feel angry and feel the desire to take action. Many feel victimized and paralyzed.

Personally, when someone I trusted pulled my job out from under me, I felt crushed, confused, disoriented. Suddenly, I discovered that my world was not what I had thought it was, and I felt cast adrift, without solid ground.

When we find ourselves in this "pocket of pain," the tendency for most of us is to get out of it as quickly as possible. We jump into another job, another relationship or another activity. We replace noise with noise, stimulation with stimulation. The quiet space of pain, failure or rejection is so very difficult to endure.

Yet, the more muscle memory we can develop to help us in confronting such situations, even if it is painful, the more likely we are to learn and grow.

LEARNING FROM OTHERS EXERCISE

If personal introspection feels too overwhelming, think of a time a friend or family member was in crisis. You may feel better equipped to scrutinize what they had to go through because you have more emotional distance from the situation. For me, helping others feels easier than helping myself, because I find it easier to feel empathy and be patient with others than with myself. I fear it's a female or learned trait, but I've learned that it's true.

As you think of how you were able to give someone else encouragement, what advice did you pass along?

• Did you try to take the pressure off, to give them time to find new strength and a more solid footing?

• Did you help them to reduce their feelings of guilt or self-blame for their situation?

• Did you offer optimism, hope and confidence that a better situation —a happier situation—was still possible?

All this was certainly helpful to the person who received your support. Recalling the ways you tried to help is a great refresher to draw on when you find yourself confronted one of your own inevitable inflection points.

CHAPTER 02

MAKE ROOM FOR IMPERFECTION

Find out who you are and be that person. That's what your soul was put on this Earth to be. Find that truth, live that truth, and everything else will come.

— ELLEN DEGENERES

FOR MANY OF US, ACKNOWLEDGING IMPERFECTION IS difficult. If we concede to ourselves that perfection is unattainable, we are admitting we do not have full control over our lives. That can be terrifying. It was a question I came to ask myself as I struggled with the realization that I wasn't Superwoman after all: Why was not being perfect more frightening for me than it seemed to be for the men I knew?

When I was a young woman, I had a male colleague with a great strategy for disarming people who might otherwise tease or criticize him. One morning, he spilled coffee on his tie right before a meeting. Instead of taking it off and running out to buy another one (as I had done a million times when my stockings developed a tear), he walked into the room and said, "OK, everyone, look at my tie. I'm a slob and spilled coffee on it. Laugh and snicker if you want. Now get over it, because I have something to say and I don't want you distracted by the brown mess near my navel." He then went on confidently to what he wanted to say.

I remember being taken aback at first by this, and then immediately feeling a little envious of his complete honesty in the moment. Would I have done the same? What is it about girls and women that makes us feel the need to hide the snag or replace the coffee-stained shirt? We seem to feel that the way we present ourselves to the world must be impeccable, and that anything less is a sign of incompetence and inadequacy—or worse, of weakness.

As Cindy Ratzlaff and Kathy Kinney, authors of *Queen of Your Own Life,* asked a group of women at the Massachusetts Conference for Women:

"Do you avoid getting together with friends because you've put on a few pounds? Do your knees shake as you obsess about the placement of every glass, dish, fork and morsel of food for holiday meals? Does a last-minute call from a friend stopping by send you dashing around the house cleaning and straightening up—even in the rooms they won't see? Are you convinced that everyone else is leading a happier life than you? If you suffer from any of the above symptoms, you may have a case of the No. 1 disease affecting women 18 to 100: perfectionism."

That may be an exaggeration, but the pursuit of perfectionism among women is widely understood to start early in life. Girls compare themselves with each other as their bodies develop at different rates. They also compare themselves with the airbrushed and genetically fortunate models who grace our magazines and media. The quest for an impossible ideal has resulted in an epidemic of eating disorders and unhealthy body images. Girlguiding UK, a leading charity designed to empower girls and young women, found that 25% of 7- to 10-year-old girls already feel the need to be perfect. According to a 2011 Seventeen/Yahoo survey, a whopping 74% of women between the ages of 13 and 21 admit to feeling that pressure to be perfect.

The statistics on this extreme focus on body image are equally disturbing. The Multi-Service Eating Disorders Association (MEDA) reports that 15% of women 17 to 24 have been diagnosed with eating disorders and 91% of female college students have attempted to control their weight through dieting. If we are hoping to raise empowered young woman, these are not encouraging trends.

I have personal experience with this drive for perfection. In high school, I did not give much thought to my weight. I received plenty of attention for a voluptuous figure that had somehow sprouted between freshman and sophomore year, to the delight (and sometimes ridicule) of my co-ed classmates. But when I got to Wellesley College, I was surrounded by 2,000 highly capable and often beautiful women. My confidence took a hard kick. The things I felt I couldn't control (or motivate myself to achieve)—being top of the class, fitting in with classmates I admired, being able to balance late-night beer and pizzas with exercise—resulted in my gaining the "freshman 20" and, in turn, losing my confidence. It also spiraled into a bout of bulimia in the second semester of my freshman year.

In those days, behavioral scientists attributed eating disorders to the search for something to control when the world around you feels uncontrollable. I am sure there is merit in that theory. For me, the eating disorder marked the beginning of my quest for perfection, the feeling that unless I was the prettiest (read: "skinniest"), as well as the smartest and the best liked, I had somehow failed. It was the beginning of my telling myself that I wasn't good enough.

PERFECTIONISM AND STANDARDS

According to some studies, this struggle to achieve perfection affects women almost twice as much as it affects men. The *Journal of Occupational and Organizational Psychology* reported in 2009 that women are more likely than men to experience feelings of inadequacy at home and at work, and that a larger proportion feel that they consistently fail to meet their own high standards.

This is not something that most women simply grow out of. It follows them through life and can get even worse when they enter the work world. Claire Shipman and Katty Kay, authors of *The Confidence Code,* note that half of female managers reported self-doubt about their performance, as compared with fewer than a third of their male counterparts. An internal survey of women working at Hewlett-Packard also found that women applied for a promotion only when they met 100% of the qualifications. Men applied when they met just 50%. My male friend's ability to recover from his coffee spill, joke about it as a distraction, and move on is a tiny example of the gap between the standards women and men tend to hold out for themselves and the confidence they possess.

Perfectionism can have serious implications beyond body image. It has been linked to anxiety and depression and the health and happiness of young women. A National Health Service study found that 28.2% of 16- to 24-year-olds in the United Kingdom have a mental health condition, with one in four women of age 16 to 24 experiencing anxiety, depression, panic disorder, phobias or obsessive-compulsive disorder.

While diagnosed cases of eating disorders are often taken seriously, given the high mortality rates with which they are associated, the dangers of perfectionism, and particularly the link to suicide, have been overlooked, partly because perfectionists are skilled at hiding their pain. Admitting to suicidal thoughts or depression doesn't fit in with the image we are trying to project.

My own belief was that the more perfect I could be, the more I would gain trust from clients, respect from peers and love from my spouse, and become a role model for my children. Boy, was I wrong! Thomas S. Greenspon, a psychologist and author of a research paper published in *Psychology in the Schools* on an "antidote to perfectionism," confirms that the most successful people in any given field are in fact less likely to be perfectionistic. Anxiety about making mistakes gets in the way of real success and advancement. We focus so much on being perfect that we miss the opportunities to see and build on our gifts.

Still, there's a distinction between perfectionism and the pursuit of excellence, Greenspon points out. Perfectionism is more than pushing yourself to do your best to achieve a goal; it's a reflection of an inner self mired in anxiety. "Perfectionistic people typically believe that they can never be good enough, that mistakes are signs of personal flaws, and that the only route to acceptability as a person is to be perfect," he writes.

The one thing these people are decidedly not perfect at, research shows, is self-compassion. Gordon Flett, a psychologist at York University in Canada who has studied perfectionists and how to help them create positive coping styles, came up with an insight that it took me years to realize for myself. In an article published by the American Psychology Association, he advises us to project this drive for achievement outside ourselves: "There is much to be said for feeling better about yourself by volunteering and making a difference in the lives of others."

As a parent, it's even more important to rein in your inner perfectionist. Research suggests that perfectionism is a trait you can pass down to your kids. Perfectionist mothers create an impossible standard for daughters who look to them for examples—something I was told directly by a psychologist who was trying to help one of my children. His observation gave me a sharp dose of humility.

One simple way to help your kids, Flett suggests, is through storytelling. "Kids love to hear a parent or teacher talk about mistakes they have made or failures that have had to overcome," he says. "This can reinforce the 'Nobody is perfect, and you don't have to be, either' theme."

There are several huge takeaways here.

FIND SELF-COMPASSION

Kristin Neff, a psychology professor at the University of Texas, is highly critical of our national quest for developing high self-esteem.

Neff echoes Greenspon, suggesting that self-compassion, rather than self-esteem, is a better path. Rather than being so hard on yourself in times of disappointment, treat yourself as you would your best friends when they screw up.

Neff says that self-compassion also involves mindfulness. We have to be willing to turn inward, be aware of our feelings and acknowledge our suffering. Typically, we don't want to do that. We want to avoid it, don't want to think about it and prefer to go straight into problem-solving.

Fortunately, mindfulness is starting to catch on even among our youth. It makes me think of a friend of mine, Hannah Manfredi, whom I met through Parlay House events. Hannah, a petite, soft-spoken young woman, teaches mindfulness to students at inner-city schools as part of her efforts to give back to her community. Her aim is to help students who might express their anxiety and stress in the form of anger and violence learn instead how to manage their feelings through mindfulness.

That generosity of spirit and action in such a young woman left a significant impression on me. I was helping mentor a young Cambodian woman, Sreileak Hour, trying to get a scholarship to an American university as part of the SHE-CAN organization. When she reached a roadblock in her path, Hannah sprang to mind. Sreileak and her family had begun to put their lives back together after the Cambodian genocide, and she was the top student in her class at school and had earned a perfect score in Cambodia's national exam. But the stress of taking the TOEFL (testing her proficiency in English as a second language) was causing her paralyzing anxiety. She had no way of dealing with her stress. Her first mediocre score threatened to undermine all her other accomplishments. My heart hurt for her, to see her come so close and yet not to be able to realize her dream.

I put the two of them in touch so that Hannah could teach Sreileak some of the basic mindfulness techniques that were so effective with the kids at her inner-city school. The two young women spoke for only 30 minutes over a crackling phone line, but something special happened. Sreileak internalized Hannah's guidance and went back the next day for her final chance to score well on the TOEFL. And she did, earning a score high enough to win a full scholarship to Scripps College in Claremont, California. Sreileak is now an A student who was accepted at the London School of Economics for her junior year abroad, and she is tutoring kids who need help in math and economics, subjects that come as naturally to her as mindfulness does for Hannah. (We will talk more about these innate strengths in Chapter 03.)

The lesson here is that mindfulness—taking stock of one's anxiety and how to cope with it—was the solution to breaking through to success.

TALKING ABOUT OUR FAILURES

Neff's insight that we tend not to want to confront our failures, and would rather go straight into problem-solving, rings true to me. As a parent, I tended to go into "strategic mode" when one of my daughters experienced a struggle. My younger daughter, Ciara, who has her graduate degree in psychology, has instinctively understood since she was a young girl the need to discuss failures. If she had a bad day at school, she would tell me about it. Dozens of times over the years, she has said to me, "Mom, I don't need you to help me fix it. I just need you to tell me you understand how bad I feel and how hard the situation is. I want empathy, not a solution."

Out of the mouth of babes.

I treated myself as I treated my daughter. I was rational and stoic rather than gentle and caretaking with myself. I look back on the years as a single mother raising my daughters and realize how rarely I came home from work and told them I was struggling. I never shared my mistakes and failures, never admitted when I felt like an outsider or didn't know what to do. I felt that if I told them I was imperfect, or that I was having difficulties, they might question my ability as a mother or have less respect for me. As a single mom, I feared my failures would worry them. I also believed that since I was the only active parent, the high bar I set for them would be the only model they had to set standards for themselves. So, I put on a brave face, rarely talked about the struggles in my day (or my life) and boxed up my self-doubt.

This did not serve them well. Because my kids saw me as ruled by perfection, they felt embarrassed or inadequate when they made mistakes, never getting the reassurance that imperfection is part and parcel of life. My daughters had no way of knowing how I was feeling, to offer me the empathy they needed themselves. Meanwhile, I had no way to face my own feelings and give myself that important self-compassion. I denied us all the opportunity to learn how to pick ourselves up, lick our wounds, and learn that we were strong enough to rise again.

In retrospect, this was a huge mistake. I now see, years later, that I learned more in the times I failed or fell short of the mark than in the times I hit 100%.

The work world was not very different in that respect. While there were many women in advertising with me, very few women had reached the top. As a CEO, I didn't want to show vulnerability or failure, for fear my male counterparts running other agencies would doubt my ability to lead. I also wanted to be a strong role model for the women coming up after me. In the wild world of advertising, talking about problems or fears without being able to provide a definitive solution was stigmatized as a sign of weakness. The less I could be truthful and vulnerable, the more I felt isolated and lonely. It led to an untenable level of stress, which I believe may have been a catalyst for the recurrence of my cancer. It was years before I could talk about my failures, asking for help on the issues I faced and including others in how to resolve them.

THE POWER OF POLARITIES

All philosophies, from the ancient Greeks to the Chinese concept of *yin* and *yang,* stress the idea that no single state can exist without its opposite. We cannot be perfect without recognizing imperfections. We cannot succeed without some measure of failure. We cannot find strength without acknowledging our weaknesses. If we make life black and white, while striving for perfection or rebounding from failure, we may be able to balance out our extremes, but we also tend to miss the gray, which is where most of our real-life experiences are situated.

I like to think now of each aspect of my own life—family, work, relationships, health and community—as operating along a horizontal wave, like a sine wave. Each aspect has its own highs and lows, and my goal is to know that over the course of my life, I will have hit highs for each one, and rebounded from lows in each one. So, at the end of my days, while I will never have been the perfect mother, the best friend, the constant work success, perfect lover or most generous philanthropist, there will be moments I can look back on and know that I did well and was strong. This feels like a much more reasonable expectation than attaining constant perfection. It is also true that when you are pushing hard to achieve success in one or two of the aspects of your life, it is impossible to do them all well at the same time. This is not a new thought: Remember the Byrds' No. 1 *Billboard* hit of Pete Seeger's song in 1965, whose lyrics came almost verbatim from *Ecclesiastes 3:1:* "To everything there is a season, and a time to every purpose under heaven."

The point is made in Disney's 2015 award-winning film *Inside Out,* in which the five emotions of Joy, Sadness, Anger, Disgust and Fear are represented in animated characters who influence the protagonist, a young girl named Riley, as she moves through her life. Disney created the film for children, but its message also resonates with adults. As the plot progresses, Joy, who has taken center stage throughout Riley's childhood, figures out that she is, in fact, not in charge and that it is Sadness who makes the very existence of Joy possible for Riley. It's a simple point, but one that we often miss: Without one end of the spectrum, we cannot experience the other.

What's the takeaway here? I believe that when we stop criticizing ourselves and practice self-compassion, we can sit with our weaknesses without losing self. Once we identify that weakness, the sense of failure or sadness helps us to feed our strengths, which helps us to deal with our challenges.

As we saw in Sreileak's case, Hannah shared her command of mindfulness to help Sreileak develop skills to cope with the stress that was getting in her way. By turning Sreileak's attention from the outcome (perfection) to the process (putting herself in the mental state to draw on what she already knew), Sreileak was able to fulfill her objective of winning a scholarship. She stopped thinking so much about the accomplishment and shifted her focus to enjoying the process. In doing so, she could relax more, observe more, and find her own strengths to pass on to others. Yet another Parlay Effect in motion.

———

As we move on to Chapter 03, where we will explore how to leverage our individual strengths, keep these points in mind:

- *Your achievements don't define you*

People-pleasing and perfectionism are your attempts to prove your worth. Underlying both is fear—fear that you're not good enough and that others will reject or abandon you. As a result, you believe you have to keep pleasing, achieving and perfecting in order for people to like and want you. You become a hamster on a wheel; you're stuck doing and doing, but no matter what you do, it will never be enough. Perfection is impossible, and pleasing everyone is impossible. This is a fact of life for everyone.

- *Other people's perceptions don't define you*

When you focus on pleasing others, your true self becomes disconnected from the self that you present to the world. You start living your life to please others or for the "gold stars" and accolades.

Not only is this tiring, but people's acceptance and love for you arises from the outward persona you're showing them, rather than from your true self. Their approval does not quiet your self-doubt and anxiety, because you still fear that people won't love and accept you for the person you are on the inside.

• *Your sense of self matters*

People-pleasing and perfectionism are like shields that hide and protect your true self. The more pleasing and perfecting you do, the more out of touch with yourself you become; you no longer know what you like, what you believe, what's important to you, or even who you are, because so much of your time and effort is spent trying to be what others want you to be and projecting an idealized version of yourself. Finding yourself can feel like a big endeavor, but you don't have to do it all at once. Bit by bit, begin to explore and experiment, constantly checking back in with yourself to see how it feels.

Try asserting your point of view in a discussion where your opinion differs from those of the other people present. See how it feels to express yourself in a way that is unusual for you but true to your real beliefs. Or try expressing yourself in a different way. If someone says something hurtful in a way that you would usually let slide (in order to seek approval or to avoid conflict), try using one word that opens up the conversation. I find that "Ouch!" is a nonconfrontational way to get started. Self-discovery is a lifelong process, because we are all constantly changing.

• *You are the boss of you*

As you let go of other people's perceptions of you, one of the biggest steps you can take is toward increasing your own positive self-talk and self-compassion. If you begin to give yourself more love and acceptance, you will become less dependent on other people for making you feel good and worthy.

Remember, it is never too late in life to learn to live with your weaknesses and to express self-compassion on the road to finding your personal strengths.

QUESTIONS TO ASK, STEPS TO TAKE:

Can you think of a time in your life when you felt stretched particularly thin and when something was asked of you that required even more of your time, effort and attention? It might be a favor for a friend, volunteering at school, helping someone in your community, or something altogether different. Now, think back. Did you:

* Accept with grace and a sense of inner peace, knowing that you had the space in your life to accept the task?

* Accept immediately and willingly because that was what was expected of you, regardless of the impact on you personally?

* Accept begrudgingly, feeling that this would be the response that was expected of you, but also that it would suck your energy and take away from your other priorities?

* Decline, trying to mark your boundaries, but feeling guilty that you could not do it all?

* Decline with a sense of self-awareness, knowing that agreeing to the request would represent too great a personal cost to you or too great a sacrifice?

When the next situation like this arises—and it will—try to get to a place where you can have the clarity to respond with either the first or the last response in the list. Both of these recognize your own needs and what you can or cannot give at this particular moment, and help you to identify and respect your boundaries.

Because, as women, we are prone to perfectionism, we are often held back both from trying new things and from advancing in our careers and in other endeavors. Think of the last time you were looking to move up, let's say at work. Did you:

• Wait until you were totally proficient at the new job before throwing your hat in the ring? If so, did waiting make you feel more secure and confident? Alternatively, did it make you feel somewhat resentful that others had not imposed the same stringent standards upon themselves?

• Did you decide to try for the advancement on the premise "Fake it till you make it"? If so, was this a comfortable step for you to take, knowing that you were going to have to learn on the job?

Of course, these are two ends of the spectrum: One is the perfectionist's stance and the other is somewhat cavalier. The next time a situation like this arises, see if you can find a way to meet in the middle: to feel confident *enough* about your skills and abilities and also take a leap of faith into the unknown. You are likely to be better prepared than you think.

CHAPTER 03

IDENTIFY YOUR STRENGTHS

Never underestimate the power of dreams and the influence of the human spirit. We are all the same in this notion: The potential for greatness lives within each of us.

— WILMA RUDOLPH

WHEN YOU WERE IN SCHOOL, YOU ASSUMED THAT THE teacher's assessment of you was always correct. The idea of being your own best advocate and forgiving your imperfections (as discussed in the last chapter) didn't align well within a learning environment where someone judged you, subject by subject, and compared you to your peers. For high achievers, it's often not the teachers' marks that drive our self-perceptions. Do you remember being a student and bringing home your report card? Did you walk in the door and think to yourself (or say to your parents), "Wow, I got an A in English! I am so proud of myself?" More often, you may have ignored the A's and focused on the B's, C's, and D's. Certainly, the F. The areas where you failed or didn't excel stood out disproportionately compared to the achievements. You judged yourself a "failure."

This pattern of focusing on areas of failure probably didn't stop when you graduated. What do you remember about your most recent performance evaluation at work? Did you feel elated about your company's recognition of your contributions, or did you play the "areas that need improvement" over and over in your head?

What about a compliment you received lately from a friend? Did her comment, "Wow, that is a really smart insight," feel like praise? Or did you take it as a sign that you rarely have had other interesting insights, and further proof that you aren't smart or valuable?

Why do women discount or ignore our successes and downplay our strengths more often than not? Why do we focus instead on the areas that are harder for us? When things go well, why do we attribute it to luck? It's likely because we have been raised in an environment where the emphasis is on what we can do better and where we have failed rather than celebrating our strengths.

Somehow, we discount what we are naturally good at, especially if it's a quality or skill that comes to us without too much work. We assume it is less valuable because we didn't have to struggle to earn it. So instead, we strive to be "well-rounded"—strong in everything— rather than determining what we are best at and learning how to build on those talents.

THE PERFECTION EXPECTATION

While some men certainly focus on their weaknesses more than their strengths, in general, men seem to feel more freedom to explore their passions without getting caught up in the expectation of succeeding on all fronts. Remember the Hewlett-Packard study (mentioned in Chapter 02) that revealed that men applied for positions when they met only 50% of the criteria required, whereas women waited until they felt perfectly qualified before applying? Steve Jobs, Mark Zuckerberg and Bill Gates all dropped out of college to pursue their passions, and didn't seem to think twice about their teachers' opinions or grades. When John Lennon was expelled from Liverpool College of Art, he didn't wallow in his academic failure. He decided to follow his strengths (and his passion) and join a band. We all know how that went.

Looking rationally at the gap between how women and men evaluate their strengths, women are more likely to strive for well-rounded perfection, whereas our male counterparts accept and focus on the things they are good at. It seems obvious that we should give ourselves the same freedom that men allow themselves. If we can spend more time building on what we do well and less time obsessing about the things that don't come as naturally, we may increase the chances that our natural abilities will form the foundation for a strong life's work.

FIND YOUR STRENGTHS

If you measure yourself by universal standards rather than by your own measurement, it's easy to miss your uniqueness. Many of us might describe ourselves as capable, but not as exceptional. Modesty may be playing a part. But for the self-critics among us, how do we know where our real talents lie if they are not obvious to us?

One valuable way of identifying our strengths is to use a validated assessment tool, of which there are plenty on the market. My favorite is the Gallup's Clifton StrengthsFinder test. This online assessment provides you with five attributes that are designed to summarize your strengths. I took the test again recently, and for people who know me, some of the results of this assessment might seem predictable. For example, it is not particularly surprising that it identified me as "Strategic." I like looking for insights and figuring out the best path to get where I am headed. Nor was the assessment that I was a "Maximizer." I have led many companies and have learned that maximizing my own achievements and those of others are key to a company's success (and that I was good at it). But then I went on in the assessment to find that I was a "Relator" and an "Arranger." Have I always had those qualities? And what do they imply? While I do not have the assessment results from the test I took more than 10 years ago, I believe that these two attributes are relatively new to me. For at least the first 30 years of my life, I was an introvert and certainly not a "Relator" who was comfortable connecting with other people. It is interesting that my insight for Parlay House (which was about how isolated women feel without having other women to connect with) helped me *relate* to them, and it then drove me to begin *arranging* ways for us all to connect. In this case, the natural strengths I had, but was unaware of, prompted me to start the organization that is the foundation for this book.

One of the great benefits of a validated assessment tool—in Gallup's case, more than 16 million people have used it—is that you can feel confident about the strengths it unearths. It opens the door for someone who might be modest or self-deprecating to stop and accept the results with "Yes, that makes sense! And I *am* strong at (fill in the blank)."

These assessments give you what I would consider a scientific way of thinking about your strengths and abilities, which is a useful place to start. Backing that up with more intuitive sources will give you additional information on the areas where you shine.

SEEK EXTERNAL FEEDBACK

In the highly collaborative world in which we live, crowdsourcing your strengths—gathering feedback from *your* personal community —is a great way to identify the ways you shine. Whether you look as far back as President Andrew Jackson's Kitchen Cabinet or the proliferation of peer advisory groups, such as Vistage, Parlay House or YPO, The Young Presidents' Organization, a network of young chief executives, it is always valuable to solicit the opinions of others around you.

I have developed a trusted circle of people in my life that I can count on for feedback and guidance, whether on relationships, job opportunities, fashion advice, financial management, health questions or charitable opportunities. I have found that soliciting second opinions from people whose experience is different from my own is exceptionally helpful and reduces the number of times I second-guess myself.

Friends have shared other informal ideas with me for gathering feedback from their inner circle. One group asked each member to come up with just one word that would describe another person in the group. Responses ranged from "funny" to "kind" to "elegant" to "there." The subject in this case shared with me that she found the last response the most meaningful: a friend who could be counted on to be "there," no matter what. Another colleague shared a tradition of her group of six women, all long-time college friends. On each woman's 50th birthday (and any birthday would do as well), they identified "the 50 things" they loved about that person. Each person contributed 10 statements, and someone compiled them in a list for the birthday girl to keep. The results were often very touching and gave the recipient a revealing overview of the actions, attitudes and strengths she had exhibited over the course of those long-term friendships. Regardless of what method you use with your group of close friends, the honest feedback you receive can be incredibly valuable for pointing to strengths and also to areas that may trip you up. One woman reported that most of her friends described her as smart and pretty, whereas at this stage of her life, she most valued the traits of kindness and warmth. It gave her food for thought about how to grow and outwardly express herself going forward.

DEFINE YOUR VALUES

Once your strengths and best traits have been identified, it's time to probe deeper. Knowing what you do well and naturally is only half of your story. The other half is what you value and how you prioritize your decisions, commitments and relationships.

Become clear about the thoughts and actions that mean most to you and determine where you are not willing to compromise. Other people may have achieved great success following a path that might feel uncomfortable to you. (Their priorities may be different from yours.) Keep in mind that your values may change over time, based on your circumstances. For example, in your early years, when you are looking to prove yourself, you may consider putting in long hours at work to demonstrate your abilities. Getting promoted, increasing your salary and achieving a level of success may be worth the trade-offs of a robust social life, leisure time or flexibility with your family down the line. (Maybe those trade-offs will never be worth it. Again, this is all about personal values.) As you age, the significance of what you choose to do or the legacy that you leave behind might be what drives your daily decision-making. Independence may become more important to you than conformity. There are not many wrong answers, except those that cause more harm than good. But clarity about your values and priorities will help you decide how to build on your strengths.

If you are not clear on what your values are, look for signs. Is there something that unexpectedly moves you? Ten years ago, I used to cry while watching the TV show "Extreme Makeover Home Edition" with my kids. I wasn't crying because I have a passion for the home-renovation business, nor did I identify with the religious undertones of the show. I was crying because the program rewarded deserving families who were not as fortunate as I was. Often, the recipients of help had given of themselves to others. Through this show, they became beneficiaries of a home renovation that allowed them to continue living their lives in a giving and loving way. I felt at the time that it seemed to be a silly thing to cry about, but in fact, it was an early sign of how actions that change the lives of others moved me. It just took me a while to figure out how to make use of this discovery in a way that felt right for me.

Maybe you have been in a similar position. You have heard about a woman who is mentoring an exchange student and thought, "I wish I had time to do something like that." You have read an article or watched a program about a movement or political issue that spoke to you on a really personal level. You have identified a problem confronting someone you care about that no one truly seems to be acting on. You resonate with a person running for political office whom you think would make a difference in your community. You notice a situation in your community that really upsets you, but no one is doing anything about it.

Once you have found your "Yes!"—something that touches you and that you would like to try to do something about—it's time to pull out that list of your personal strengths and values.

FIND ROLE MODELS

As we found in our Parlay Effect research, sometimes the road to finding our strengths is to receive inspiration from others. We found that witnesses of supportive actions feel empowered as a result of having been encouraged, and then chose to pass on encouragement or coaching to another person.

I am sure we can all think of someone in our life whom we admire greatly and from whom we draw strength. If you feel a connection to or similarities with certain people, do a deep-dive into the things you like in them, to see whether their techniques and approaches might benefit you. See where they apply similar skills to yours and determine whether a comparable application might work for you.

If possible, turn them into your mentors. Bounce ideas off them, mirror them or just observe them in action.

Someone whom I don't personally know, but who continues to inspire me, is Brandon Stanton, author of the Instagram sensation (and now best-selling book series) *Humans of New York*. He started as an "average observer of people," inspired by the unexpected lessons he learned from everyday people he would see on the streets of his hometown. Through his photography and interviews on social media, readers had a window into the inspiration, passion, quirks, resiliency, honesty and real-life experience of his subjects. Some were moving, some amusing, and many gave an illuminating glimpse into the life of someone whom most of us wouldn't have noticed while walking full speed through our lives. The relevance and meaning of their experiences became a reminder to many of us of our shared humanity, and sometimes the stories prompted action that led to empathy, kindness, forgiveness, generosity and inclusion. Brandon's work was one of the stimuli that encouraged me to start Parlay House. I was first an observer, then a conduit for sharing personal stories that unite us.

FIND YOUR FLOW

Once you have determined your strengths, defined your values and identified role models who can serve as beacons for you, it's time to pull these insights together. When that happens, at whatever level, you can think of it as "finding your flow."

Mihaly Csikszentmihalyi, professor of psychology and management at Claremont Graduate University and author of the best-selling book "Flow," describes flow as "a state of heightened focus and immersion in activities such as art, play and work." Performers, athletes and everyday people will tell you there is nothing like this feeling of being at one with the world when you are caught up in it; it is the ultimate expression of our strengths at work. We are so perfectly aligned with who we are and what we care about that the actions feel effortless, and time often passes as though we were in a meditative trance.

I am often in a state of flow at Parlay House events, when my natural skills at relating and arranging make the evening fly by. Three hours can feel like 15 minutes, and I can't believe it when the bubbling guests say it is time for them to go. Before I founded Parlay House, it had been a long time since I had experienced that feeling. Perhaps the last time was in high school, when I was lost in time and space, designing and sewing clothing for myself. My other friends didn't sew, but my passion for fashion and design, and my desire to create something unique and meaningful to wear to school the next day, had me up until 3 or 4 a.m. without even realizing that the time had passed. I was simply caught up in the process of creating.

Once you find your flow, you will be at the intersection of what you do well and what you are passionate about, and then you can jump in, to take real action. My philosophy for people trying to test and experiment to find their flow can be summed up in this simple motto: "Keep saying yes until you have to say no." Keep experimenting in small ways, saying yes to ideas and opportunities, until it is very clear that what you are doing is not building on your strengths or passions, or is not aligning with your values. This operates on the assumption that you will find flow not only by staying open to a myriad of possibilities but also through signs that you're not in your element. One thing is certain: Flow cannot be forced.

FIND YOUR SUPERPOWER

There is a big difference between trying to play Superwoman and finding your own superpower. Superwoman, who expertly manages a home, brings up children and pursues a full-time, high-powered career, is nothing but a myth. Moreover, trying to become Superwoman can cost you, big time: It means applying a sense of drive to every aspect of your life, and becoming a slave to the to-do list. Some of us relish this feeling of busyness. It is proof that we are competent and needed, capable of doing and being so many things to so many people.

The problem is that it's difficult to stay present with those around you when you are checking boxes of activity all day. It's also impossible to care for yourself when you don't have a shred of free time. Then, when a major stumbling block hits and lands you at rock bottom, suddenly the Superwoman you thought you were collapses, destroyed by the reality of your human flaws and imperfections, which loom large in times of failure, struggle and disappointment. We learn, to our cost, that striving for impossible perfection and achievement in all aspects of our lives can actually work against us and sabotage our real potential.

Each of us, though, has "superpowers," and finding them is our formula for having meaningful impact in the world.

FORMULA FOR SUCCESS:
STRENGTHS x VALUES = PERSONAL SUPERPOWER

A superpower is defined as a "power greater in scope and magnitude than that which is considered natural or has previously existed." Your superpowers may not feel super to you. That's because they build on who you are, tapping the natural strengths that have been part of you for so long that you are no longer really aware of them. When you leverage those strengths and put them into action in the service of your passions, however, you create a formula for progress and impact. Women who can find their superpower have the ability to rise above challenging circumstances and change lives.

I noted in the last chapter that Steve Jobs, Mark Zuckerberg and Bill Gates dropped out of college but went on to achieve phenomenal success. They didn't worry about being well-rounded or how others graded them. What if I told you that Ellen DeGeneres, Oprah Winfrey and Lady Gaga also dropped out of school? They too have shaped their own lives. Oprah soared by taking her television format into new territory of transformation and motivation. Ellen rose not only because she is a great comedian, but because she was brave and highly effective in framing a new way for a gay woman to do comedy, based on a personal mantra of "being kind to one another." Lady Gaga not only tapped into her gifts as a singer and performer, but took her teenage experience of feeling like an outsider and used it to appeal to a huge range of young people—including those who feel as isolated as she did. She had an uncanny ability to reach out to unique individuals who may not conform to the norm but who can find a sense of pride in their individuality. Each of these people who made their own way to the top were able to keep in touch with their superpowers, a combination of their strengths, values and passion.

THE STRENGTH OF WOMEN

Returning to the widely used Clifton StrengthsFinder (Gallup) tool, it is interesting to note the precise nature of women's strengths. Gallup found that women share four of the five top strengths with men—Learner, Responsibility, Relator and Input—but the fifth strength distinguishes the two genders. Men round out as Achievers, whereas women round out with Empathy. In my view, this distinction can be used effectively to create meaningful change. Empathy involves an intimate awareness of others, while achievement is about relative success. Gallup's findings suggest that, by comparison with men, women are generally more inclined to focus on groups or teams and to explore what it means to work in collaboration with others. Women tend to be more sensitive and intuitive to what is going on with the people around them. Men, on the other hand, are more apt to gather external data and internalize their decision-making. Rather than asking for feedback from others, men tend to look for answers from within.

It is important to note that these discoveries apply to men and women in general and do not apply to individual men and women. Differences are much greater within genders than between genders. The takeaway is that if women are set up to empathize—to include and to embrace others—the Parlay Effect has enormous innate potential.

QUESTIONS TO ASK, STEPS TO TAKE:

As we've discussed in this chapter, it's often hard for us as women to identify our own strengths. It is not in our nature, as a general rule. But let's start to change that. If you were to list your strengths, how easy would it be for you to do so? Would you, for instance, be able to describe yourself in five key words? If so, do that now. Carry those words in your wallet or enter them into a note on your phone. Add to them as you become aware of more.

If this seems like a stretch, I encourage you to seek outside sources:

1. **Use a validated assessment tool.** There are many to choose from, including StrengthsFinder 2.0 (my favorite), VIA Inventory, Strength-scope, Strengths Profiler and others. The idea is to simply try one and see how the results hit you. Sometimes the information will seem quite straightforward, but you may be surprised what these tools unearth about your hidden talents.

2. **Get feedback from friends, family and colleagues.** You can do this in a number of ways. Think of the people in your life who know you well and whom you can trust with your most vulnerable self. Ask each of them to give you a few words or phrases that best describe your strengths as they see them. Then supplement those attributes with what you have learned from job reviews, family feedback or other experiences where people summed up what they felt about your strengths. Look only for patterns and repetitions of the positive traits that seem to be apparent to people in a broad range of relationships with you. These are likely to be things that people have said to you, like "I can always count on you to..." or "You have a gift of..."

As for finding role models, see if you can identify a role model in your life who:

- knows her strengths and her superpower
- is willing to risk trying something new even if she is not 100% qualified for the "step up" out of the gate
- is generous with others in terms of advice and support, passing along what she's learned for the next wave of talent.

If you are lucky enough to have found this role model in one person, good for you; follow her path! What's more likely is that you admire the strengths of a number of people. You can create your own composite role model by combining them. Do not be afraid to include male role models and advisers in your portfolio as well. Throughout my career, I've encountered men who set examples I could emulate and taught me approaches to life from which I could benefit.

CHAPTER 04

REDEFINE
RECIPROCITY

I've learned that people will forget what you said, people will forget what you did, but people will never forget how you made them feel.

— MAYA ANGELOU

WHEN I FOUNDED PARLAY HOUSE IN 2012, I WAS DIRECTLY addressing the fact that I felt very alone at this new stage in my life. I had moved to a new city and left my work and friendships behind, and my daughters were off at college. While long-distance communications remained, I needed to figure out how to create a new cadence to my life and find a new focus that built on my skills and strengths. It was time to find the intersection of what I do best and what I am passionate about.

I experimented at first by putting my fingers into a lot of different pots. I directed a program at Stanford University that focused on helping college students develop and maintain a healthy body image. I volunteered with a number of nonprofit organizations supporting women. I mentored a few young adults. I continued serving on the boards I was committed to. All of these things were interesting and different, but with a consistent thread throughout.

When I looked for commonalities among them, the answer was clear and simple: I was most excited about the personal interactions I had within each of these endeavors.

Researchers and academics who study "dislocation," that is, the loneliness I was feeling when I lost my job and my health, have written about the importance of personal connection. Bruce Alexander, professor emeritus at Simon Fraser University, spent a lot of time studying the effects of loneliness and isolation on both animals and humans. One branch of his research included the issue of drug addiction and whether it was associated with loneliness. Like many scientists, he started his research first by observing rats and then testing his observations with human subjects.

He first studied whether a rat, alone in a cage, would choose to drink plain water or water laced with an addictive drug like cocaine. The lone rat invariably chose the cocaine water.

Then, something surprising happened. When additional rats were introduced into the cage, both the old rat and his new rat friends chose to drink the plain water rather than the water with cocaine. The rats were happier being with each other, and lost the desire for the extra stimulation of the drug.

Not surprisingly, this experiment played out similarly with humans.

As another example, in a 2015 TED Talk at TEDGlobal/London, Johann Hari cited the example of research presented in the *Archives of General Psychiatry* that studied soldiers who had served in the Vietnam War, 20% of whom were estimated to be using heroin in combat. When they returned home and bonded with other healthy, happy people, the number of heroin users dropped dramatically. Research has found that the antidote to addiction is connection. Humans want to bond with each other by nature, and it is when they feel dislocated that they start to unravel.

QUALITY OVER QUANTITY

We know that not all connections are meaningful. For example, when you are looking for a new job or are working in a field where the people you know can make all the difference, you are likely to spend time collecting business cards and making connections. When I was running advertising agencies, I was "friends" with hundreds and even thousands of employees and clients in the industry. But when I lost my job and no longer had immediate power and influence, I discovered that the number of true friends I had was negligible. My work connections had been mostly transactional in nature: "What can you do for me?" Or: "If I do this for you, you will owe me going forward."

Look at the success of LinkedIn, Twitter and other social platforms that allow you to expand your reach in quantity and breadth of connections. They can be transformational for people looking for reach within the business world, for sure, but they are also very oriented toward metrics: Adding more people to your network is the be-all and end-all.

Unfortunately, most of the time, those sites are not conducive to building profound relationships. The trick is to be able to distinguish between networking and connecting. Be careful not to confuse the two. Networking often means putting forward a "marketing version" of how you want to be seen, while connecting means getting comfortable enough to reveal your deeper self. In my view, networking is "going wide" while connecting is "going deep." Knowing yourself and what you value will give you the confidence to distinguish between the two, as well as to be open enough to truly connect.

I have found that my circle of 20 close friends are willing to extend generosity to me to a far greater extent than the thousands I am "networked" with on social platforms. Both have value; it's simply important to distinguish between the two.

MATCHING BRAINWAVES ARE REAL

Putting yourself out there with others is a hard thing to do. Moran Cerf, a neuroscientist at Northwestern University who has been researching how people make decisions for over a decade, concludes that the most important factor when you decide to extend yourself is not the topic or idea you choose to pursue but the person with whom you choose to be.

His research found that when two people are in each other's company, their brainwaves will begin to look nearly identical. "The more we study engagement, we see time and again that just being next to certain people actually aligns your brain with them," Cerf says, based on their mannerisms, the smell of the room, the noise level and many other factors. "This means the people you hang out with actually have an impact on your engagement with reality, beyond what you can explain. And one of the effects is: You become alike." This may very well help to explain the force of peer pressure! It also gives us clues about whom to associate with and spend time with as adults. And it also explains why some friends finish each other's sentences or order the same items on the dinner menu.

Cerf's observations remind me of the African proverb: "If you want to go fast, go alone. If you want to go far, go together." Since the brainwaves of people who are together tend to align, even being with another person can create a chain of connections that have meaning and impact.

THE RIGHT CONNECTIONS: TAKERS, MATCHERS, GIVERS

If you have been wondering how to put yourself forward in something that is truly significant to you, it's often easier when you can find another person or a couple of people who share some of your values and goals. This not only allows you to feel a greater connection with a small community of other people but can give you a sense of momentum. As we found in our Parlay Effect research, initiators found a surprising sense of community. It made them feel part of something bigger. And recipients felt "seen" in a way that made them feel more relevant, included and subsequently more empowered to act themselves.

As you look to increase your impact, how do you find people with whom one plus one results in something more powerful than two? How do you know where to dig deep, with whom to partner and where there are people you can trust?

In his book *Give and Take,* Wharton professor Adam Grant groups people into three types: Takers, Matchers and Givers.

He summarizes:

1. Takers try to get as much as possible from others.

2. Matchers try to trade evenly.

3. Givers tend to contribute to others without the expectation of anything in return.

You probably know a bunch of "takers"—it's hard not to encounter these folks in life. These are the people who appear to be new friends and ask you out for lunch. Shortly after the main dish arrives, you find out they actually aren't interested in being your friend. Instead, they need a favor, a donation or some information that will help them. "Takers" might be the parents of one of your child's friends, who have let their child come to your house for play dates, sleepover weekends and family movie night, but have never offered to host your children. Or the business associate who never reaches for the check after lunch, despite the fact that you are on the same salary level. These people are not your potential partners for beginning chain reactions for good. In fact, if you aren't careful, they will try to make themselves the recipients of your good intentions.

The "matchers" are a bit more interesting. Their operating style comes from something familiar to most of us—the Golden Rule of doing unto others as you would have them do unto you. If you help them by giving a recommendation to their child who is applying to your alma mater, they will invite you to another event that you might enjoy. If they step in to bring the kids home from soccer practice, they expect that you'll pick the gang up the following week. Their operating system is one of generosity—in the expectation of payback.

My experience is that "matchers," people who act with the expectation of reciprocity, are the norm and represent the largest and most common bucket of behavior. Following the Golden Rule, they look to exchange favors with each other for mutual benefit or for the promise of returning the favor in the long term.

There is nothing wrong with matchers, except to note that they, too, involve you in transactional relationships. While someone may take action to benefit others, they are operating on the inherent assumption that they can expect the recipient to return the favor in the future. If the good deed is ultimately not reciprocated, the relationship usually weakens or peters out.

Finally, there are the "givers." Givers are not as selfless as they may seem, but unlike the matchers, who work to return the favor for everything done on their behalf, givers measure "payback" as the good feeling that comes from the act of doing something for someone else. People who are givers seem to be able to act with no thought of what is in it for them or any expectation of reciprocity.

Grant notes that givers can be taken advantage of in society and, in the workplace, may lag behind those who break out of the box early by "taking" and "matching." The long-term prospects, however, are far greater for givers, he notes. Being a giver in your life doesn't mean that you have to sacrifice self-advocacy at work, although it can admittedly be harder for givers. We are all, after all, multifaceted.

WHAT MAKES GIVERS ABLE TO GIVE?

Researchers have studied for some time the motivational factors behind the practice of giving. Lara Aknin, a researcher at Simon Fraser

University, found that even in young children, the act of giving, especially when this meant giving away something special, generated greater feelings of pleasure than receiving it themselves.

In one of her experiments, toddlers were asked to share a treat with a stuffed animal, a cute monkey puppet. They were told that the puppet really liked eating treats. The children were then given some of these treats for themselves. The researchers viewed the videotapes of the sessions and coded the children's faces for their positive emotions. The toddlers, who were far too young to understand the idea of generosity, smiled significantly more, it turned out, when they were giving treats away than when they received an identical treat from the experimenter. Giving up something that belonged to them, their own treasure, is what seemed to make the children happiest.

Aknin found similar results in experiments with adults. She recruited a sample of students in the morning hours on campus, giving them a small amount of money, from $5 to $20, to spend that day. She and her colleagues broke them into two groups, asking the members of one group to spend the money on themselves and the other to spend it on someone else. At the end of the day, she called them back to see how they were feeling. She found that people who were randomly assigned to spend the money on others reported that they were significantly happier than those who had spent it on themselves.

These results, across the populations of both children and adults, underscore that most of us have a natural inclination to give. The question of whether one embraces the role of being a giver, however, remains open. Why do some follow through on this tendency, while others do not? I believe that givers possess three traits in greater depth than people who are matchers: empathy, generosity and, surprisingly, humility.

Empathy, which allows someone to put themselves in the shoes of another person, is what helps us to relate to each other. We feel compelled to understand their emotional state, what they are feeling and what they need in the situation.

Generosity is what prompts them to act, to give of themselves, drawing on their natural strengths, a fortunate life situation, or a lesson from a past experience that can help to alleviate the burden for someone else. Givers do it in without thought or expectation of anything in return.

Humility, the third trait, is more complex. Humility is defined by social scientists as "a core psychological process theoretically marked by low self-focus, secure identity and balanced awareness of strengths and weaknesses." They think of it as two components—an intrapersonal one and an interpersonal one. A number of scientific researchers have suggested that humble people are able to maintain a more accurate view of their relative strengths and weaknesses than those who seem filled with overt confidence. The speculation is that humbleness allows them to be oriented towards others rather than self-focused, and they are therefore able to regulate their egos and cultivate interdependent relationships.

Humble individuals are confident in themselves—aware of and at peace with their strengths and weaknesses. This enables them to orient themselves towards others rather than focus on themselves. As a result, their confidence increases—confidence that they have something to give, confidence in their values, confidence in their strengths and confidence in their ability to take risks without worrying about failure.

A ROLE MODEL OF GIVING

Vicky Tsai, a dear friend and the founder of the now nationally success-ful cosmetics brand Tatcha, attributes her success to learning from someone whose life has been steeped in giving, despite the fact that his means are limited and his reach is narrow.

Vicky describes the first decade of her career as "Death by a thousand cuts." She and her husband, Eric, both traders in credit derivatives, were at their desks at the World Trade Center on September 11, 2001. When the Twin Towers fell, she realized that her outlook had changed radically and that in her mid-30s, she was no longer the "shiny, happy 21-year-old" she had once been.

In crisis, she quit her job, knowing that she was disappointing her parents, who had come to the United States from China two years before her birth in order to give her every advantage. But she just wasn't able to continue anymore on her initial career track, and she took time off to reflect and to find a new path. Picking up odd jobs, such as working as her apartment building's superintendent, she earned enough to travel throughout Europe and Asia. Her only goals while traveling were to listen, learn, explore—and be inspired. Maybe she would find something to give herself new direction.

When she found herself in Kyoto, Japan, Vicky was entranced by the cobblestone streets, canals lined with cherry blossoms and radiant gold-leaf temples. Her hotel hired her a taxi driver, who not only drove Vicky to temples, markets and botanical gardens, but also gave her nature and history lessons. The driver's name was Toide-san, and Vicky describes him as a tall teddy bear of a man with kind, soulful eyes. He acted as more of a learned guide than a driver, and Vicky marveled that he knew so much more about true service than many of the highly trained people she knew back home.

Toide-san's pride in his city and profession was captivating, distracting Vicky from the other big life event she was grappling with: her first trimester of pregnancy. Struggling with morning sickness, she asked Toide-san to pull over every few blocks so she could be sick. By midday, she felt so terrible that she asked him to take her back to her hotel so she could sleep.

Vicky awoke in the late afternoon to find a package waiting for her in the lobby. She was puzzled because she knew no one in Kyoto. Opening it up, she found three CDs filled with photos of Kyoto, with a note from Toide-san. Instead of taking a job that afternoon to earn the income he sorely needed, he had chosen instead to exemplify a selfless Japanese tradition called *"ichi-go, ichi-e,"* which literally means "one time, one meeting." *Ichi-go, ichi-e* expresses the Japanese cultural concept of treasuring one's meetings with people. After meeting Vicky and understanding both her mission and her plight, he had gone home so he could compile and share with Vicky photos of his beloved city that he had taken over the years. He even included a photo of Vicky from that morning, which he made into the CD covers. She smiled as she imagined him cutting the photo into those perfect CD-sized circles, and marveled at the magical images that filled the gaps of the tour she'd so desperately wanted to take.

"That gesture was the kindest thing anyone had done for me in years," Vicky recalls fondly. Toide-san's generosity launched a cascade of subsequent events.

Vicky's time in Kyoto restored her faith in humanity, and inspired her to start her own beauty company, Tatcha Cosmetics. Beauty had always been a passion of hers. Toide-san's kindness, and learning about the beauty regimen of geishas whom she met later on her journey made her see that she could translate this grace into products for others.

"Toide-san embodied a value system that is still everywhere in Japan: that honor, service and artistry still matter, and that every interaction is a gift," Vicky says. "I wanted to create a company to bring those values to the world."

Toide-san's images were the first used on the company website, and still appear in Tatcha materials to this day. His attitude of service informs everything Tatcha does, as the fastest-growing independent beauty company in the United States today. One example: Rather than customer service representatives, Tatcha has a "customer love team" to create a genuine relationship with clients.

Vicky still considers Toide-san a dear friend, connecting him to every employee and friend who visits Kyoto. "My dream for Tatcha is to bring this kind man's dedication to *ichi-go, ichi-e* to people around the world," she says. "If I'm very lucky, perhaps we are touching other people's lives with kindness the way he touched mine."

FINDING WHAT WE HAVE IN COMMON

It is interesting to note that Vicky had not only made a connection with another person when she met Toide-san, but that she also made a connection with a city. Kyoto was a place that she found beautiful and safe, inspiring and aspirational.

When I founded Parlay House, I had no idea that creating a safe and inspiring physical space would be important. But it turns out that creating a familiar venue, especially a safe space like a home, is a great way to reduce the anxiety of people who have a hard time opening up. What's more, inviting people into the place where you live, especially when you don't know them, is unusual in our society. We invite intimate friends to our homes. We invite family. We invite close business associates. But we don't invite strangers. It turns out that Parlay House should have been called Parlay Home, because the significance of making people feel welcomed, on a trusting and personal footing, is one of its biggest draws.

When I launched Parlay House in New York City—where people are quite selective and private about how they entertain—members of Parlay House could not believe that I would invite strangers into my apartment. Even more than the speakers who addressed us or the connections they made with other women, the fact that I was so open attracted attention. Trust engenders trust, and openness fosters more openness.

Shared space and shared experiences create familiar territory for everyone, and this is a great way to find commonalities to break the ice at the start. As experiences are shared, trust increases, and it's easier to find shared truths.

Toide-san recognized the many ways that he and Vicky were different. But he also saw the many things they shared. That transition from "How are we different?" to "What do we have in common?" was crucial in his finding a way to begin a cascade of kindness that animates Tatcha.

The fact that Toide-san is a man is also important. While I believe that as women we are empowered by other women, there is no reason that enlightened men cannot participate in such outpourings of positive change. While women score higher on the empathy scale as a general rule, male figures have also empowered, coached and supported us. Their role cannot be dismissed, and we cannot lose sight of this opportunity. Those of us who are mothers of sons can help encourage them to become adults who are comfortable partnering with strong women. This is crucial to our ongoing growth. I know that my sisters and I would not have become the strong women that we are without a father who knew that we would become strong and confident women capable of doing whatever we wanted.

Toide-san and Vicky are only one example of personal connections that are not based on reciprocity, but on generosity and understanding the value of a single human interaction. I watch similar cascades of commonality at Parlay House gatherings on a regular basis.

With the organization's thousands of members across San Francisco and New York City, it is impossible for me to remember details about the members whom I don't know well. But by being a good listener and observer, I have often found that after chatting separately with a couple of different women, I notice that they seem to have a "similar vibe" or have expressed interest in a generally similar subject. After introducing them to each other and including the observation that I think they have a lot in common, I have been amazed by the intense connection and intimacy that they seem to find. Their connection blossoms based on *my* assertion and *their* assumption that they share many common interests. This is how I originally envisioned the Parlay Effect in its purest form.

The genetic differences between individual humans today are minuscule—there is about 0.1% of variation between us. Similarly, as women, our life experiences, personalities, interests and passions may be very different, but we have far more in common than we might imagine. Those shared truths, similarities and aspirations are strengthened in each of us when we find others like us.

In her journal, Frida Kahlo wrote:

> I used to think I was the strangest person in the world but then I thought there are so many people in the world, there must be someone just like me who feels bizarre and flawed in the same ways I do. I would imagine her, and imagine that she must be out there thinking of me too. Well, I hope that if you are out there and read this and know that, yes, it's true I'm here, and I'm just as strange as you.

I have a painting of Frida in my living room, which was created by an artist who used these words in color blocks to create her image. It serves as a reminder to me personally, and a reminder to our groups as a whole how bizarre and different each of us feels. Yet when her words come together to form an image, and when we come together to become a living organism that is listening to someone's life story and finding common connections between unlikely friends, magic happens.

This commonality, I believe, is what will allow us to do something fundamentally different as we meet each other. It will allow us not to see what we can take from each other, or even what we can do for each other. Our commonality will allow us to see how, one to one, we can create something that ripples outward, something that is not about reciprocity or what will come back to us but rather about kindness, connection, generosity, coaching or empathy that will support the next woman. The warm feeling that you have when you know that you have done something for someone else, and how that can spread outward, is the Parlay Effect.

QUESTIONS TO ASK, STEPS TO TAKE:

Only you can know your patterns and intended behavior—whether you are more of a taker, a matcher or a giver. I know I'm biased in my perspective, but it does seem to me that givers not only have more to offer those around them, but feel better about themselves in the giving. At least that's true for me.

If you want to take simple steps to become more of a giver, here are some suggestions:

• Put yourself in someone else's shoes. Come up with an unexpected way to do something that you think would help her. Do it without being asked to or without expecting to be recognized for your actions. Do it anonymously if you can, to separate the gesture from any response from the recipient.

• The next time you feel you need something and begin to reach out to ask someone to make a connection for you, stop and think for a moment. Have you asked a lot of this person lately? Is there another way to find what you need? In this relationship, have you been more on the giving or on the receiving side? It's not bad to ask for help, but it's good to take an honest look at the balance.

- Check yourself on your tendency to exchange favors. Do you have friends whom you go out of your way to help, but whom you resent because they are not as thoughtful or helpful in return? The best way to change this dynamic is not by doing less or expecting more, but by releasing your desire for reciprocity and just feeling good about your role in the giving.

CHAPTER 05

TAKE NOTICE
OF OTHERS

*She is a friend of mine. She gather me, man. The pieces
I am, she gather them and give them back to me in all the
right order. It's good, you know, when you got a woman who
is a friend of your mind.*

— TONI MORRISON

AT THE END OF EACH PARLAY HOUSE SESSION, THE WOMEN
who walk in the door are not those that walk out again. Even if the
shift is small, something happens in the two hours we are together.
I have witnessed it time and time again. I believe this shift occurs for
two reasons. The first is that at these events, we share stories. Some
of them involve great trials that are difficult to hear. When women
do take them in, it is impossible not to be moved in one direction or

another. The second is that when women are in a room, we notice each other. We've been socialized to do so, perhaps not always in positive ways, but we are trained in what I call "the art of noticing." Used constructively, this can be a valuable asset.

When I talk about the "art of noticing," I don't usually mean the physical noticing with which we are all familiar—commenting on another woman's necklace or asking about her haircut, although these casual observations can be helpful as a way to begin a conversation. Therapists often use this technique to build trust and start sessions on a positive note. I am not talking about noticing people physically. I am talking about "emotional noticing."

I break down "noticing" into a series of steps that build from an awareness of yourself and how you feel in the moment to an awareness of others, which leads to a true ability to connect with them.

FIRST, NOTICE YOURSELF

You've already learned how to be aware of your strengths and interests. But are they apparent to others? How are you putting yourself forward? It's easy to assume that what you feel, who you are, your experiences and your greatest passions are clear to those around you. After all, it's clear to you! But the reality is that your style and presentation may cloud other people's ability to see you the way you really are.

In earlier chapters, we focused on getting to know our own strengths and finding our passions. But working on how we communicate those strengths and passions and how to put ourselves into situations where we can be better understood will allow us to relate to people who want to do complementary things or with different people whose diversity of thoughts, experiences and ideas are enriching to us.

Here are some ways to accomplish that:

* *Be conscious of the tone you strike*

Make sure that what you are projecting is how you want to be seen. When I was a CEO, my kids would call me at the office, and if I didn't know that they were on the line (this was in the days before caller ID), I might answer as I would to a client, or my boss at corporate HQ, or some other business associate—in a commanding tone that I felt was appropriate in a corporate context. I never understood what my kids meant when they said that my voice scared them and that they wanted Mommy back. I was not consciously aware that the calm, nurturing self I projected when I was with them was completely different from the leader I needed to be at work. I tried to project blue skies to the kids and confidence in midst of the storm to the business world. Both of those projections were intentional and authentic but represented different parts of myself. It is important to be aware of what we are trying to convey and whom we are trying to reach, if we are to be perceived as we intend.

* *Create a personal comfort zone*

To be comfortable enough to connect with yourself and those around you, you need to find a way to see and be seen that is true to who you are. For example, I am an introvert by nature, much more comfortable with one-on-one conversations than in big groups of people where the conversations seem more superficial. I love leading teams, but for many years I was somewhat tentative when I spoke to the company or in larger groups, because I was just plain shy. For the first 10 years I found myself in a leadership position, I had to act as if I loved speaking publicly until it finally became true and more natural to me. It took a lot of practicing and reframing before I mastered it.

Ultimately, I found my comfort zone, an authentic way of making speeches. I started by practicing and acting "as if," and later by adopting a style of speaking through storytelling. When I am happiest communicating, it feels as though I am talking to a single individual, even if I am talking to a large crowd of people. Speaking by way of storytelling is my way of bringing intimacy to wider settings and projecting myself as I want to be seen.

- *Reveal your self-awareness to others*

It's very easy to look at other people's lives and think they have it much easier than you do. Sometimes that may be true, but more often than not, the happy and successful lives people present at gatherings and through social media are not the real story—or at least not the full story. Everyone around you has a history of struggles and failures, learning moments and missed opportunities. We are all judged, and often incorrectly. Some of the misjudgment is easy to understand; very few people talk about their moments of struggle, insecurity or failure. When they meet you, they don't talk about feeling anxious, being fired or that they are unhappy with the way their body looks. They don't start saying that they are worried about paying the mortgage. There is no reason they should reveal their insecurities and fears unless they want to. But you should recognize that if people are only sharing the happy moments, you probably are not getting the full story.

As I've gotten older and more relaxed in my imperfect skin, I have become more at ease in talking about my mistakes and failures. But you don't need to talk about yours unless you are comfortable doing so. What you can do, however, is to draw on the hard moments and missed opportunities and use them to your advantage. Times of struggle or pain are perfect opportunities for gaining self-awareness. Sometimes these periods are a sign that you are not in tune with your strengths and your passions. Sometimes this is just bad luck and sometimes, you just plain failed. But the failures do provide context and perspective. We all struggle, suffer loss, feel pain and miss goals, and without those lows, we would never be able to experience the contrasting highs: success, insight, happiness and love.

When you feel stressed, it's very hard to be aware of what you are projecting. You might be feeling anxious and it may seem to other people that you are disengaged and aloof. Or you may be angry about something related to work, and it gets carried into a family environment where the anger is displaced onto those around you. It happens to all of us, but self-awareness will reduce the number of times we are misunderstood.

In challenging circumstances, I find it helpful to share with people that I am "not myself today." Give those around you a cue that you know you are feeling out of sorts. The acknowledgment isn't permission to let loose your feelings onto others, nor does it require that you talk to them about the pain you feel. But giving them a cue is a good way to let them know that you are aware of your unusual behavior and that its cause has nothing to do with them.

SECOND, NOTICE THE PEOPLE AROUND YOU

I vividly remember a particular Parlay House event. I was immediately drawn to one of our new guests. Bubbly and outgoing, full of confidence, Heather Jerrehian told me she was born in San Francisco, and I assumed that she always had lived in the Bay Area. At one of our first gatherings, she volunteered to help me develop the Parlay House brand. I saw Heather as someone who really had it together and could make things happen in the world. I took notice of her, or at least I thought I had.

Years later, Heather told me her real story, the one I did not hear that day.

2009 was the worst year of her life. Heather and her business partner had just somewhat reluctantly sold their "baby," The Proportion of Blu, a premium denim jean company that they'd built from the ground up. Sadly, the buyer closed the company a year later, sweeping away the blood, sweat and tears Heather had put into building it.

To add insult to injury, Heather finalized her divorce the same year, dashing her dreams of living happily ever after. In her words, "No white picket fence and no children, because I had been too busy working to get ahead."

Heather did find a way to reinvent herself. She moved to the East Coast and started an organic farm. She speaks of it as the deepest and darkest year of her life, but one that provided the perfect environment for life-altering personal growth.

Three years later, once the farm was up and running, Heather says she felt the deep sadness begin to lift and a new life emerge. She decided to return to the Bay Area, and was introduced to Parlay House through a friend. When I met her that day, she still had the wounds from these experiences that she had tucked inside, but all I noticed was the outgoing persona she brought to our gathering.

This was her authentic self, for sure, but there was far more to learn. Once she shared with me her struggles and pains, I appreciated her all that much more. I decided going forward not to judge only the public persona, but to truly *notice* others. Seeing people's authentic selves, even in their vulnerabilities, can strengthen your connection to them and the choices you make in that relationship.

THIRD, NOTICE WHAT HAPPENS
WHEN YOU EXTEND YOURSELF

In most situations, when you gather the courage and energy to do something with someone outside your usual circle, one plus one will equal more than two. We found very clearly in our Parlay Effect research that people who were initiators of a helpful/kind/generous act inspired a chain reaction of connection and kindness. In Heather's case, she found new connections, both personal and professional, when she put herself forward, even when she didn't feel like it. Meeting new people resulted in leads, invitations and new relationships for her, as well as newfound comfort in having a safe place where she could be herself.

If we are truly to appreciate others, we need to feel safe. Simply noticing other people is not the same as "vigilance"—a state of high alert. Noticing requires a level of calm and safety. For me, Parlay House was the venue. But women have many ways to create, as leaders, or to join, as participants, communities where genuine relationships can develop.

You might want to create your own version of Parlay House. In the Epilogue, I offer some guidance on how to approach this. Organizing content-based events on an ongoing basis may require too much effort to start with. Less ambitious versions of this same idea—creating a space where you can feel comfortable in your human imperfection and open to others, can happen in a group that meets for lunch on an ongoing basis. Book or movie clubs, where the reading material opens up a discussion, are great ways to connect and to find what you have in common. Volunteer projects about things that are important to you, such as working in a homeless shelter serving food, helping to rebuild a community playground, or reading books to kids at a local library, are likely to introduce you to people who share your passions and interests. Look for an environment that lets you be yourself and to find opportunities to start significant conversations with others.

THE ART OF LISTENING

The art of listening plays an important role in nearly all forms of human interaction. In the business world, the companies that listen best are often the most successful. Listening to employees helps to create a work environment that offers greater employee satisfaction and, as a result, higher productivity, retention rates, creativity and more. Better listening to customers, often through technology, is consistently connected to business growth and increased profitability.

As individuals, we don't have an algorithm or technology that listens for us. We all want to be heard, and to rise above the din of social media to feel genuinely understood. We don't always have control, though, over how others will receive the information we are putting out.

In *The Lost Art of Listening*, Michael P. Nichols, Ph.D., points out that "the yearning to be heard is a yearning to escape our isolation and bridge the space that separates us." Feeling "unheard" and isolated was exactly what led me to develop ways to connect with other women, and to create Parlay House. His observation resonates with me.

But how do we become good listeners? Dr. Nichols suggests that empathy is at the heart of good listening skills. When we stop thinking about what we ourselves are trying to say or what we are thinking, and hear what someone else is trying to communicate, it builds trust. Trust then allows the person being heard to feel safe and connected to the listener. Trust cements connections and fortifies the sense of self of the person being heard, as well as of the person listening.

It's not always easy to set aside our own need to communicate and to listen to someone else. But if we do so, we are taking their feelings and needs seriously. After a while, we may start to wonder, "Where is the room for my feelings?" As Dr. Nichols says, "It hurts not to be listened to."

In serious relationships, an imbalance of listening is likely to result in an erosion of trust. But in new relationships, I believe that by temporarily putting aside your needs and being genuinely attentive to a new person, she or he is likely to feel heard. Being heard, they will feel valued, noticed, and drawn to you as a result. It's a great way to open the door to real dialogue and a terrific way to know where the other person is coming from, so that you can discover what you each have in common.

THINGS ARE NOT ALWAYS AS THEY APPEAR

Heather's story of overcoming adversity caught me by surprise. My assumption observing her was that she was a well-put-together woman whose life had been easy. I had seen her as self-assured and carefree, but I had not listened deeply enough to learn her underlying story of struggle and pain. Certainly, she hid it well, but I missed the opportunity to listen to her because I didn't think to question my first impression.

Heather presented herself as she wanted to be seen, and she revealed the story of her struggles only to people she felt she could trust, when it felt safe for her. Her experiences of failure and loss were real, and her experiences of picking herself up and starting again gave her long-term faith in her ability to rise above exceptional circumstances.

My friend Kevin Chatman followed a different path, but his story, in terms of self-reflection and choices, has fascinating parallels with Heather's. His mother raised him and his brothers in a crime-infested neighborhood in San Jose, California. She did her very best to keep her kids out of trouble, but the pull of the streets and the easy availability of drugs led Kevin away from his mom and in a dangerous direction. After two violent crimes as a teenager, he committed a nonviolent crime as a young man. This "third strike" meant that he would be sentenced to multiple life sentences in prison under the state's stringent three strikes law.

Then, in 2012, the law was amended, allowing for the reassessment of third-strike prisoners and their sentences. Kevin became a free man. Being free was a gift, but being free was hard. Kevin had to figure out how to re-enter society and avoid being drawn back into his old neighborhood. This is when I met him. I was the executive director of a documentary film called *The Return,* a story about prisoners returning to society after serving long prison sentences. We contacted Kevin in the hope that we could follow his journey and help to reveal how difficult the path to re-entry really is, and how we as a society fail to support people who are coming out of prison. Understanding the significance of our topic but fearing that he might mess up again, Kevin reluctantly agreed.

Kevin found the process of being filmed uncomfortable. The segments following him showed him reporting to his parole officer to be tested for drugs and making intimate visits to his dying mother, which left him feeling exposed and vulnerable. The film also showed his decision to choose transitional housing based on a religion different from the one that had helped him become straight. But he bared his life and soul in our film, and he began to heal. It was a cathartic time for him, and one he hoped would represent another step on a solid road forward.

The film went on to be nominated for an Emmy and continues to reach thousands of people, first on PBS and now on Netflix. Kevin is now part of the touring production team and answers questions from the audience after film screenings. This often includes people who know someone caught up in the unforgiving prison system. Kevin takes the time to speak to, and more important, to listen to, every person who comes to him. Many feel isolation, shame and despair as a result of their own experience with the prison system. Recently, he told me about an email he received that is typical of the recurring conversations he has:

My name is Mike, and we met a couple of weeks ago at the screening of The Return. *I wanted to share something very personal with you; I believe that when you spoke with my dad, he shared that he had also served a short sentence in jail. This is something we hardly ever spoke about in my family, especially my dad, as he saw it as one of the lowest points in his life. But after meeting you, he started opening up for the first time. Over the course of the following days, he repeatedly said that this was the first time that he was able to recognize his strengths in coming out of jail, rather than just looking at his failures, which put him in there. There was a real healing that happened there, which allowed him to finally come to terms with that part of his past.*

In Kevin's second chance at life, he has become a spokesperson for other formerly incarcerated people, raising awareness of the need for support services, housing and employment for them upon their release. His bravery in revealing his journey, his failures as well as his triumphs, has helped people who have been holding onto secrets to find their voice and hope for the future. He has become an advocate for others and opened a dialogue on a topic that society seldom discusses.

Crossing paths with Kevin—and recognizing his arduous journey—makes it far easier for me to tackle the challenges in front of me. "If he can do this, I can do this," I have said to myself repeatedly.

———————

It's an interesting formula: "Identify Your Strengths" (Chapter 03) plus "Redefine Reciprocity" (Chapter 04) often results in a "Taking Notice of Others" (Chapter 05).

Unlike Kevin or Heather, many of us don't have a huge, life-shattering event that forces us into a major shift in perspective. Without that impetus, what do you do if you know you want to take action in some way, but don't know where to start? It's easy to get into a rhythm of life where the familiar, everyday business of life takes over, and we stop looking for ways to create change.

Fortunately, I've now seen that small things can also have much broader consequences. You don't need a major trauma to start a cascade. The art of listening alone can spark a change. As our research shows, being a witness to an act of kindness can spur you to initiate an act of kindness. This can start when you give someone else time to be heard, or you open yourself up to the option of helping them. The listening alone may lift a burden that frees them to be able to move forward in their own way. And listening to them may awaken you to a feeling or an opportunity you might not have anticipated.

It is usually impossible to track the exact chain of events that happen from these connections, but it's clear from our research and my own observations and stories that they cause a ripple effect of kindness and empathy that does not stop at the recipient. The Parlay Effect flows to the next woman, to the next and to the one after that.

It is important to remind ourselves that these connections are not always reciprocal—they are not the exchanges of people trading favors. These are chain reactions of one woman providing something that another woman needs—empathy, comfort, encouragement, validation or something more tangible, like coaching or a referral. What I have witnessed at Parlay House gatherings is that in an environment of trust, a series of bonds, activities and initiatives happens as a result of women sharing truths. As they feel connected and empowered, they pull other women into our circle, and the relationships grow outward.

QUESTIONS TO ASK, STEPS TO TAKE:

This chapter has been all about the art of noticing and listening. We often think that people with personal power or strength know how to instinctively step into a situation and take command. They may walk into a room and take charge or have a personality that seems bigger than life. The truth is, people in positions of true strength have done a lot of noticing and a lot of listening on their path to success.

To get started, try this experiment: The next time you are in a situation where you feel you could step in right away to solve a problem or represent a point of view, wait a little, and do these things first:

• Notice what is going on around you. Who is holding back, who is speaking up, and why? Notice the feeling in the room: joyful, tense, conflict-ridden, resigned? What information is available and what has not yet been uncovered or offered up? Make a practice of this type of noticing *before* you speak or act.

• Listen, really listen, to those around you. The best leaders, especially those in new positions, come in with an open mind to learn. Listening is critical to learning, as is the humility to understand we cannot be masters at everything out of the gate. Making a practice of listening before speaking and acting will make your strengths even more effective, especially when you decide to use them for the benefit of others.

Experiencing a shift in perspective—a way to see something anew or from a different angle—can often save us in times of despair. Is there a moment in your past when you were going through a very difficult time, an illness or depression, a sense of loneliness, some type of loss, a challenge that seemed insurmountable? Chances are you felt very alone in that experience. The next time you find yourself in such a situation, see if you can do one of two things:

1. Find others who are experiencing something similar. This could mean seeking out a support group where members share their experiences. Just hearing other people describe a similar situation can help you turn your feeling of loneliness into togetherness. The challenge may remain, but you are not alone in facing it.

2. Share your struggles with a friend or several close friends. Chances are you that will soon find you are not alone. Or you will hear a story of someone else who is experiencing something as hard or harder than what you are facing. We often become convinced that our pain is uniquely overwhelming until we hear the story of another person who is braving something far worse. Feeling grateful despite our own misfortune can offer an enormous boost.

CHAPTER 06

SEIZE YOUR CONFIDENCE

The truth is: Belonging starts with self-acceptance. Your level of belonging, in fact, can never be greater than your level of self-acceptance, because believing that you're enough is what gives you the courage to be authentic, vulnerable and imperfect.

— BRENÉ BROWN

IN 2015, I HAD THE PLEASURE OF SPEAKING AT THE Watermark Conference for Women. The keynote speaker was Hillary Clinton. Hillary was powerful, for sure. But it was her warm-up act, the amazingly brave, open and authentic social scientist Brené Brown, who captured my heart.

In my talk, I had been very open about the trifecta of challenges in my life—of being diagnosed with cancer, becoming an empty nester, and losing my job all at once—which propelled me to reconsider my life and eventually to start Parlay House. I felt I was candid with the audience, and that they connected with my story. But Brené's talk took openness, vulnerability and authenticity to a new level. As she put it, "When you get to a place where you understand that love and belonging, your worthiness, is a birthright and not something you have to earn, anything is possible."

This struck a chord with me. Confidence comes from acknowledging that we cannot be perfect. This idea is counterintuitive and certainly not what most of us have been conditioned to think. In fact, we feel that the more perfect we are, the more our confidence will rise. What Brené revealed to me is that the opposite is true: Many women are so set on achieving, or at least projecting, perfection, that we miss many opportunities to acknowledge our imperfection and gain confidence as a result. The authors Katty Kay and Claire Shipman underscore this point in *The Confidence Code,* saying, "In the most basic terms, what we [women] need to do is start acting and risking and failing. …Women are so keen to get everything just right that we are terrified of getting something wrong. But, if we don't start taking risks, we will never reach the next level."

PRACTICE TAKING RISKS

In Chapters 02 and 03, we talked extensively about our imperfections and the inclination of women to project an image of perfection. As individuals, women generally don't embrace risk and failure.

Research suggests that men, on the whole, tend to be much greater risk-takers than women. Some of that risky behavior expresses itself as physical, some as financial. Testosterone is a primary driver of such risk-taking behavior.

Biology and chemistry has always to some extent driven the differences in our comfort with risk. Historically, this has influenced our roles in the family unit and factored into risk-taking behavior. Men, with their higher levels of testosterone, were the providers: hunting and killing animals in ancient times, and as primary bread-winners just a generation ago. They had to take physical risks or the family might starve. Women were the protectors of the family, defenders of the household and pillars of the community. That "protection" mode put women in a more defensive (and possibly more risk-averse) posture.

But fast-forward to now, when women make up 51% of the workforce and both parents are working in a majority of two-parent households. Doug Sundheim, in an article in the Harvard Business Review, suggests that measuring risk-aversion and risk-taking behaviors on more traditional gender scales skews the results. Accounting for the circumstances of today, women are equal players. "[Traditional metrics] don't point to risks like standing up for what's right in the face of opposition, or taking the ethical path when there's pressure to stray—important risks that I've found women are particularly strong at taking," he says. The assessment of women's willingness to take risks has historically been viewed through a business or a financial lens, rather than through a social one, missing examples of risk-taking in ways that were equally daring and had a wide-ranging impact.

PRACTICE FAILING

Eleanor Roosevelt was known to say, "Do one thing every day that scares you." She knew that along with trying new things came the very real possibility of failure, and that not trying new things came with the very real possibility of stagnation.

The idea of failing over and over again is not appealing to most of us. We try to teach our children to succeed, we try to protect them from repeat failures, we emphasize learning from our mistakes, and so on. But there is a way to fail that's productive. Ashley Good, a Toronto-based entrepreneur, has built a thriving business by helping people and organizations take failures and turn them into opportunities for growth. She calls the company and the philosophy Fail Forward, and it operates on the conviction that creating work environments where there is room to try out new ideas—and to fail—is crucial to accelerated growth and innovation "Intelligent failure" is a way of reframing risk in a way that makes trying and failing a mandatory part of the process of evolution.

The same reframing can help us as individuals, and especially as women, to view failures as proof that we are trying and learning, rather than proof that we somehow aren't good enough.

So, how do we practice failing?

START BY SAYING YES

Remember Heather's story? Something she said really resonated with me: "Mine was not an overnight journey, and it was a hard-fought battle to find my way back. Going from a sense of not knowing who I was to becoming at home with myself once again took a lot of courage and perseverance. I had to show up when I didn't feel like it or felt like the worst person on this earth. I had to face rejection and failure, only to get up and try it again. Building my network took a very concentrated effort of saying yes to events, coffees and conferences across many different groups, as well as being willing to give my time and help others. It has been a long-term investment, where I am now able to share the dividends of this experience with so many others."

In other words, Heather kept saying yes to new interactions with others, despite her initial reluctance. This recalls the phrase I passed on to many friends, family members, mentees and audiences: The secret to growth is to keep saying yes, unless the no is too loud to ignore. Many of you will relate to this from the perspective of dating —it's worth giving people a few tries before it becomes clear that the symbiosis isn't there. You say yes to the second and third date, even when the first one isn't perfect. Human beings are complex, and it is worth giving new relationships a shot and getting to know each other before you decide that there are too many points of incompatibility to continue.

The same is true of developing your own sense of self, especially as it relates to new activities, friendships, hobbies and activism. Thomas Friedman, in his book *Thank You for Being Late* writes, "One way to reinforce and scale the character-building norms of healthy communities is by showing people the joys and the fruits that come from joining hearts, souls and hands—what happens when we don't just not do unto others but actually do with others in ways that are big and hard and make a difference."

DON'T GO ALONE

"Not doing unto others, but doing with others" is another way to reassess the concept of reciprocity. When we are all in it together, pulling those around us up and forward, it creates a meaningful momentum and gives us courage.

Veronika Scott is a courageous woman who knows the importance of being helped, and also of helping others. A child of poverty and addiction whose family was "very, very close" to homelessness several times, she almost flunked out of sixth grade until her maternal grandfather intervened. "He sat me down and pushed me to rise above my circumstances and become the person I was capable of being," she said. Because of her grandparents' personal investment in her, Veronika kept saying yes to opportunities to do well at school. She participated in activities and became the best version of herself, despite the intense pressures around her. She went on to earn a scholarship to Detroit's College for Creative Studies—and that's where she began helping others who were struggling with the poverty that had plagued her family and with the proximity to homelessness they all faced.

As a product design student at the college, Veronika was inspired to create something to help homeless people: She designed a jacket that was water-resistant, warm, easy to carry and could be converted to a sleeping bag. Having grown up with so little, she says, "I wanted to make a coat that wasn't someone else's trash or hand-me-down, and would give someone a sense of dignity."

The jacket not only earned her class credit but launched her on a mission in life. When she graduated in 2011, rather than going to work at a paying job, as virtually everyone advised her to do, she started her own nonprofit, the Empowerment Plan. "I'd been raised in somebody else's rock-bottom situation, so I figured even if it didn't work out, the worst that would happen is that I would be broke and still living with my grandparents." As always, they were supportive of her plans. They said, "We're proud of you."

The jackets were a great product, but Veronika saw even more opportunities to help others become as self-sufficient as she was. At 27, she had employed more than 40 people—all of whom were homeless when they were hired, and all of whom have dependents who no longer have to worry about being steeped in poverty for the rest of their lives.

"Our biggest goal is to be a stepping stone for our employees, from being in a shelter to being financially independent," she says. "From 3 to 5 p.m. every workday, our employees study for the GED, learn financial literacy, work on their résumés and do other things that make them more employable."

Rather than pity the homeless, like most people, Veronika practices a more positive approach. "Look, you do not get to pity my team!" she says. "Because, frankly, they have been through things that most people would never imagine, and they have come out the other side stronger. They are not to be pitied; they are to be admired. They are, frankly, bad-ass."

Just as her grandparents gave her hope and courage, Veronika has given hope to dozens of others through her nonprofit, which has far exceeded the reach of a class project. It has become a way to empower others to pull themselves—and their children—out of the cycle of poverty. Veronica raised herself into a position of strength and confidence by saying yes in her early years, thanks to the encouragement of her grandparents, and thanks to the permission they gave her to try, fail, and try again. She went on to establish an organization that helped people with very few opportunities find something to which they could say yes and build their own sense of self. She had a dream and made it happen, one step at a time.

FIND A ROLE MODEL

Confidence also comes through finding people we admire, in my case someone like Brené Brown, and emulating some of their behavior. First, strive to understand their thinking and actions, and then find ways to continue that ripple effect outward. Just because you didn't think of an idea that someone else may be known for doesn't mean that it isn't true for you, too. Brené is considered the expert on the power of expressing vulnerability, but it doesn't mean others shouldn't be talking about such an important topic. Once I was comfortable talking about my struggles (and how I felt even stronger after disappointment or failure), I also gained confidence in revealing my story to others so that they could know they were not alone.

As I took the risk and revealed elements of my story, I learned that my failures, setbacks and mistakes made me more approachable and identifiable. Exposing my heart and my hurt has become a bridge for the people I talk with to feel safe exposing their own vulnerabilities. When I speak openly, other women begin telling me their own stories of risk-taking, failure, resilience and success. My vulnerability helps free them to be vulnerable too. It creates a chain reaction. Of course, when I reveal my inner self, I do not always get the result I expect or hope for. Some people take advantage of my openness, or respond, consciously or unconsciously, with comments that hurt me or bring back some of my own feelings of failure or self-doubt. Some are uncomfortable because my willingness to talk openly about personal things feels like "too much information" for them. But such responses are infrequent, and the value I find in connecting with others by being vulnerable and authentic more than compensates for the few times it backfires.

When I tell my story or reveal a failure to another woman, I can't always judge the effect it has. I can tell that the other person hears me and that she identifies based on our interaction, but what she does with it involves a leap of faith. I often learn later, from stories told long after our conversations, that showing my vulnerability has energized the recipient and motivated her to do the same for another woman. It all starts with taking a risk.

STARTING THE CASCADE

As the mother of two daughters, I have been keenly aware of the messages we send our girls as they grow into women, and the messages that we women send to each other. On this topic of confidence, I'd like to offer a few things to keep in mind, especially if you are a parent, thinking of having children, or becoming a mentor. The young women of today are the Parlay Effect instigators of our future.

OFFER MANY OPPORTUNITIES FOR RISK

If you are raising or overseeing young children, you instinctively try to protect them. "Don't climb too high" is a natural maternal reaction prompted by our desire to protect our children from getting hurt. But unless the risk they are taking is life-threatening or highly dangerous, letting them climb high will teach them that they are able to climb back down. If they are afraid to get their feet wet in the ocean, ask them to tell you how the sand feels and how it changes. This will encourage them to take the risk while focusing on another aspect of the experience that scared them.

The same is true for young adults. Jumping into full-time jobs isn't always easy. Encourage them to try new experiences through part-time gigs, volunteer opportunities and internships. These are easy ways for them to dip their toes into the work world, get a sense of themselves in new environments, and build skills and relationships that will increase their confidence for more ambitious adventures later on.

My daughter Lauren, not a natural risk-taker, had a passion for young children that often took her out of her comfort zone. When our school in Uganda needed assistant teachers for basic English and math, my shy 17-year-old focused on her desire to help children, quelling her fear of traveling to Africa on her own. She focused on her passion as a distraction from her fear of taking on more than she could handle.

My daughter Ciara needed to find a way to earn income while attending graduate school full time. She invested herself in one of her side passions, being a makeup artist, and launched a freelance business. Working freelance taught her how to speak up for herself, to build a business, to manage time and commitments, to absorb disappointments, and to budget both time and money and learn that success (and lack of clients) balance out over the long term. It was a short-term exploration, but one that equipped her well as she builds her own psychotherapy practice.

LET THEM FAIL—WITH BOUNDARIES

Boundaries provide safety. The people you are mentoring need to recognize where their "No" is. I always said to my kids, "Try everything that is even slightly interesting. But if you get into a situation where you feel you have lost control, or that the risk is too great, you can use me as an excuse." Helping them prepare a bailout plan based on their own boundaries before they set out to try new things allows them to start without as much trepidation. It eased their anxiety and allowed them to get involved in activities and friendships that are beyond their experience.

TEACH THEM RESILIENCY

Teaching resiliency is easier said than done. I have found that it is often best learned through experience, and that you can't simply tell someone how to become resilient. As loving mothers and mentors, our reaction is to pick up the fallen child, to rescue the student doing poorly in a class, to solve a friend's relationship issues, or to cover for a struggling colleague. But when we do that, we deprive them of the opportunity to learn how to find inner strength and to gain confidence by overcoming a problem.

You can certainly model resiliency by talking about your own failures and disappointments, including what you learned and what you will do differently the next time. I like to emphasize that getting through difficult times, for example surviving an abusive relationship and coping with cancer, as well as smaller setbacks, like losing a job or a friendship, increased my confidence that I could handle the bumps on the road to come.

MODEL EMPATHY AND SERVICE

More than five years ago, I was the chairman and CEO of a company in turnaround. I was trying to perform my role and to remain an inspirational and empathetic leader. Unfortunately, the truth about running a turnaround is that it often requires layoffs and means saying goodbye to really good people. When we were unable to retain clients and had no option but downsizing, I was crushed. I knew each of the employees we were letting go, and what the loss of a job would mean to them and to their families. I knew the state of the economy and how difficult it would be for them to find other jobs. Visualizing how they would cope was truly upsetting.

Yet, as the CEO, delivering profit to our parent company was part of my job, and sometimes layoffs became an unavoidable financial imperative. To this day, I revisit, and regret, how I was obliged to handle this, because it wasn't in keeping with my core values. For legal reasons, our HR department gave me and all of the senior leaders scripts detailing what we could say and what we couldn't say as we spoke to each person. We were told that there was no room to say "I'm sorry." We were prohibited from uttering anything that could give an employee any reason for a lawsuit. I felt real sadness for the people I was letting go, but I was told by our legal team that I could not empathize or express regret. Of course, most of the people who were fired, many whom I considered friends, never spoke to me after they were terminated.

Janine Serio, a hugely talented art director who I had mentored over the years, was on that list. With our budgets slashed by clients, we could not retain her. I was devastated to let go of someone who had become more like a sister than an employee, and to have to do it in a way that was opposed to my values.

Recently, through social media, Janine reached out to me, having read about my sister's Letter Farmer business. She has a stationery company as a side gig, and she was impressed to learn what my sister was doing—and told me so. This launched a dialogue with her that I was now able to have because I had passed the time frame that legally bound me to the guidance of my former employer. I could tell her how highly I thought of her and how sorry I was that the prescribed process for letting her go did not allow for humanity, empathy and a real dialogue. It had not allowed me to say that I was sorry, that I believed in her, or to tell her how talented I thought she was and how much I enjoyed working with her. Not only did this recent conversation make me feel better because I was expressing my real feelings and reawakening a friendship, but it made her feel better to receive the acknowledgment and the apology, even though it was years after the event.

What I didn't anticipate was that our reconnection did more than that. When I said that I knew how much it had hurt her and how I wished I had ignored the stringent HR rules and expressed what I really felt, she responded that she was now in a senior position and that just last week, she had had to do just the same thing to another female art director who worked for her. "I'm going to reach out to her now, and say to her what you just said to me," she wrote. This realignment of my values caused a real Parlay Effect, as one woman reached out to another and tried to improve her experience.

Both women lost their jobs. Nothing feels good about that. But how they were treated and how they felt as a result of the acknowledgment helped them process and move forward with greater self-esteem, strength and confidence.

HELP THEM DREAM

T.E. Lawrence, who became known as Lawrence of Arabia, said: "Those who dream by night in the dusty recesses of their minds will wake in the day to find that all was vanity; but the dreamers of the day are dangerous people, for they may act their dream with open eyes, and make it possible."

Veronika was a "dreamer by day"—someone who saw something in the world around her and dreamed of addressing it. She put one foot in front of another to make it happen. One success led to the next, and her confidence increased. This path was grounded in her childhood, thanks to the grandparents who encouraged her and offered her ways to dream. Veronika remained faithful to her passions, in reaching out to people like her family, and developing her strengths in creativity and design. Helping other people avoid the path her family had been on inspired her.

SAYING YES TOGETHER

One of our recent Parlay House events featured four women who had met each other as expatriates in Hong Kong as they followed their husbands in their careers. They connected because they were not working, or because they felt that their careers had stagnated and were no longer exciting and fulfilling. They talked to the Parlay House attendees about how they had made a pact with each other to help each member develop her new life goals and to hold her accountable (through ongoing meetings, work sessions and get-to-gethers), so that she could make the transition she wanted to make. They called their project a "RE Group," based on the ideas of re-evaluating, reframing, reconnecting and reactivating.

Lena Cheng, a successful physician and member of Doctors on Demand, was in the Parlay House audience that night. It might have seemed at the time that the panel discussion was not relevant to her, as a professional with an impressive career. But like many of us, Lena had grown out of her role and was contemplating her next move. Hearing how these women had come together to encourage each other to reach and grow in her own way gave Lena insight into how to do it for herself: She would not go alone.

After the Parlay House session, Lena launched her own version of RE Group, combing through her personal contacts and inviting any interested Parlay House member to join her in a project of "Renewal and Reinvention." Her project was to form her own small group of women, who would gather to focus on the theme of renewal and reinvention. Here's how she described it:

MISSION STATEMENT:

A fun, creative and energetic think tank and support group for local women who are going through or desire a change or readjustment in their career or life purpose. We'll meet on a weekly basis to discuss/

challenge/encourage/share resources and hold each other accountable to the current path and/or action items we decide important for ourselves as individuals.

GUIDING PRINCIPLES:

1.   Each of us is on our own journey to find our purpose and passion. We provide a welcoming, open, collaborative environment with no pressure except that which we put on ourselves.

2.   There is strength in numbers. We come together, not only to help ourselves as individuals, but to support others in their goals and aspirations.

3.   We support each other in a positive manner, but with honest feedback for potential improvement.

4.   Group dynamics can be a challenge sometimes. As much as possible, we will work under decisions based on consensus for those that affect the group as a whole. Everyone has a voice.

5.   WE HAVE FUN and celebrate victories, small and large!"

The result of women pulling other women forward has been life-changing for Lena. Two weeks after sending out her mission statement, she organized a group of nine women who meet each Tuesday to explore, reinvent and reinvigorate each other. They have read two books together: *The Artist's Way* by Julia Cameron and *Designing Your Life: Build a Life That Works for You* by Bill Burnett.

Some of the results she reports (the names have been changed) are:

1.   Beth was stuck in a job she hated (her words!) and felt hopeless about finding a way out. She put together a plan of action, gave notice at work, and is now exploring the idea of starting her own company.

Importantly, she has increased peace of mind and feels empowered by taking control of her career.

2.   Moira was an executive at a successful start-up and resigned last year to care for an ill family member. She was able to take time to reconnect with her values and personal vision. Along the way, she connected with a friend who shares her value system, and she now works at her friend's company as the chief financial officer.

3.   Allison was in a strategy role at Tom Ford International, but was feeling restless and unfulfilled. In April, she gave her notice and is now taking some time off to decompress and consider her next career adventure.

4.   Colleen retired last year as the in-house attorney for a local city government. She was contemplating indefinite retirement but felt herself missing the intellectual stimulation and structure. She experienced a series of synchronistic moments and now finds herself about to join a law firm where she will do work she likes, have flexible hours and work from home.

5.   Lilly has a background in marketing but has always had a passion for art. She's currently exploring different career paths in public art and has rediscovered certain parts of her creative self through *The Artist's Way*.

Then there's Lena. She left her job and has taken time to rediscover joy and contemplate what she was seeking in her next chapter. After meeting with dozens of people and companies, she finally decided to join a company where she could draw upon both her medical expertise and her passion for marketing. So far, it has been a great fit.

Lena recently wrote to me and said, "The RE Group has been such a blessing throughout the last several months, as I've healed from my last job and encountered the ups and downs of a job search. And it's been tremendously rewarding to watch the other women go through their own transformations. Starting this group has been such an incredible blessing. I'm so thankful I went to that Parlay House event in January, which by itself was an act of synchronicity, because I hadn't attended Parlay House in about 18 months. Thank you again for your support and well wishes. The power of RE is alive and thriving."

———————

Ultimately, seizing your confidence amounts to finding your yes—stepping on from what makes it possible for you to show up for what is next for you and make it happen. Sometimes you can do it alone, and sometimes courage comes in numbers. There is no wrong answer.

This call to action, small and large, is what creates the kind of movement that can turn the tide for women in sustainable, irreversible and empowering ways.

———————

QUESTIONS TO ASK, STEPS TO TAKE:

What's your personal risk profile? Are you often open to trying new things, or do you seek comfort in the known and familiar?

For risk-takers: For people who are open to trying new things, people on the leading edge of experimentation, the following exercise can be helpful:

Think of one of your greatest failures and consider the following questions:

* When you failed, what happened? Did everything fall apart?

- Can you think about failures in the context of the lessons learned that actually made you stronger?
- When you were failing, did you find any coping mechanisms that helped you feel a bit more at peace with the process?

For the security-minded: For those of us, on the other hand, who seek comfort in the familiar, who worry about giving up certainty in exchange for possibility, these questions could be more helpful:

Think back on a pivotal moment in your life, a consequential one that required you to decide which way you would go, and what action you might take. Then ask yourself:

- Did I take the path that required the least amount of risk?
- Did I choose the direction that ensured my success, playing safely within my own boundaries?

If you answered yes to one or both questions above, then ask yourself:

- How might I have chosen differently, with the idea of trying something new or just for the sake of learning?
- What is my comfort level with taking a risk and not knowing the outcome?
- What does the idea of risk feel like in your body? Does it make you feel anxious or uncomfortable, or eager and excited?

In this chapter, we've discussed the value of saying yes together. Think of a group of women with whom you share a bond. It could be at work, in your community, a book club, a nonprofit where you volunteer, your church, etc. The next time you are together, think of talking with them about individual goals and how you can support each other. Even if the individual risks are small, engaging them within a safe group and getting their support during the process will help reduce the fear.

CHAPTER 07

FIND THE INTERSECTION OF POWER AND PASSION

Every great dream begins with a dreamer. Always remember, you have within you the strength, the patience and the passion to reach for the stars to change the world.

— HARRIET TUBMAN

NO MANUAL EXISTS ON HOW TO PUSH YOURSELF OUT OF your comfort zone. But in order to try new things, meet new people and, I hope, find the intersection between your prowess and your passion, you have to start somewhere.

For Tiffany Shlain, a filmmaker focused on making values-based change, her starting point originated in a family tradition. When she and her siblings were young, their parents established a ritual of going out to the movies every Sunday, followed by dinner and ice cream. While they ate, their parents would "not so subtly," as she puts it, stimulate conversation about the film, current events, and, as Tiffany recalls it, the "meaning of life." This experience stuck with her, and when she went to college, she began taking courses in film and film history.

As she took the range of required and optional courses for her major, she learned that film wasn't her only strength; in fact, she was torn between her passion for the arts and her natural interest and curiosity about technology. She calls herself "pre-Web," meaning that she grew up during a time when computers had just begun to be integrated into our lives. The World Wide Web didn't yet exist. Vacillating about which direction to take in her studies and in her life, Tiffany accepted jobs in the world of technology and then used her income to finance her films. For her, technology was interesting and came naturally, while making films was a personally challenging and ultimately more fulfilling experience. The safety of an income gave her the freedom to express herself creatively as well as philosophically.

After a few years of working in tech to sustain her films, Tiffany's world flipped. She noticed, more and more, that great creative work was not only happening in film but also in technology, where creativity could reach audiences with important messages. This was long before the days of YouTube, blockbusters and Amazon/Netflix original series. Yet at this point, few recognized the potential of the Web for its creativity, meaning and impact. Recognizing its importance, she created the Webby Awards, to honor pioneers in technology each year. Tiffany was among the few people at the time who saw the power of the Web as a platform that would become as powerful as film or television. Fortunately for her, her "safety net" of technology became her next place for creative expression.

LAUNCH TRIAL BALLOONS

We are not all like Tiffany. If you don't have a natural passion or family tradition to point you in the right direction, it's hard to know where to start. If that's the case for you, I suggest the following approach: Go wide and then go deep.

By going wide, I am referring to casting a wide net: dipping your toe into a large number of opportunities that you think you might be interested in and where you know you can make a contribution. Pick as many as 12 events in a given year (one per month is a good goal, then adjust the commitment to fit your life) to get a broad range of exposure to topics, movements and organizations that would benefit from some of the things that you do well naturally. You do not need to know how much you care about the cause or issue when you start out, only that you have some small way to contribute and some vague sense of curiosity. "Going wide" is a way to try things out and see whether there are issues you identify with, people you feel connected to or outcomes that give you the impetus to invest more of yourself.

Whether you start with an interest, an ideal, or in reaction to something that really bothers you, the cue that you are on the right track will be when you start to feel connections and friendships forming with people who share your interests. Or when something new piques your curiosity. You can then begin to focus on those areas. Over time, you will transition from trying a wide range of many things at a relatively shallow level to knowing where you are interested in doing more, learning more and giving more. Launching 12 trial balloons might develop into one or two interests, projects or issues for you. You'll shift from going wide to going deep. Personally, while being on boards gives me a great view of companies and an ability to contribute at the 30,000-foot level, seeing the impact I can have on women, either in one-on-one relationships or by creating events that turn into connections between others is where I choose to go deep most of the time. But there is no wrong answer; it's a personal choice where you choose to make an impact.

TRY ON SOME 'POSSIBLE SELVES'

"Possible selves" is a wonderful, powerful and psychologically fruitful concept.

Possible selves are the selves you believe you might become in the near future, and vital in goal-setting and motivation. Possible selves can be positive or negative: Each of us has both positive images of the self we desire and expect to become, and negative images of the self we would like to avoid. A current self-concept focuses on who one is now, or who we think we ought to be. Focusing on the future, possible selves allow for self-improvement, flexibility and personal growth. Experimenting with possible selves provides a chance to experiment with various potential futures. You might wonder: "Maybe I'll be a teacher, or maybe I'll help shape our government. What would it be like to become a teacher or a political figure? How would I get there? What are the stages and obstacles along the way?" The future is the target of much of our efforts as individuals. Homework is done (and the proverbial broccoli is eaten), all in pursuit of some potential personal self.

Why does it matter that we have these images and thoughts about ourselves, which may or may not come to pass? Well, these possibilities we think exist for ourselves can and often do influence choices, feelings, behavior and decisions in the present. Take, for example, the person who dreams of being a mother one day. To achieve this hoped-for self, she is likely to make (or at least want to make) decisions about her relationships, health and social life that are likely to result in her goal. Alternatively, imagine the person who fears being "just like her mother"—you can imagine how that might influence the ways she raises her own children today.

In short, possible selves can have enormous motivational power.

Beyond the impetus to achieve a goal that imagining our possible selves can offer, what I find particularly wonderful about it is, quite literally, the opportunities it opens up. So, if you are a stage that you can't quite imagine a path yet, go ahead and try on a few hats—a few personas—and see how they look to you.

FOLLOW THE LEAD

If launching trial balloons or trying on possible selves seems abstract, and you don't know where to start in your personal exploration, try following the lead of someone you admire. She (or he, for that matter) might be someone you know, someone in the public sphere, or even a historical figure. Eleanor Roosevelt is a role model for me. While she lived long before my time, her courageous willingness to try things that she was afraid of, and her progressive embrace of a broad range of people, have served as guiding principles for me throughout my life. I might not have given up my dynamic career to move across the country to start over again, if I hadn't felt emboldened by what she represented.

As I mentioned in the last chapter, I have also followed the lead of Brené Brown, who, by example, showed me how to be open about my vulnerabilities and mistakes. Watching her, I learned how being vulnerable could make me more approachable, authentic and trusted by others, and as a result, I have been able to connect with people at deep and significant levels.

Taking a completely different approach, I have begun to take cues from people whose styles are very different from mine but whose ideals are similar. Nancy Lublin, founder of Dress for Success and Crisis Text Line, spoke recently to a gathering of Parlay House women in New York. Her advice on discovering where you can make an impact was not to emulate others or to follow a passion, but to ask yourself what really makes you indignant. Are there situations that you find exceptionally frustrating or worse? Nancy finds that working to solve a problem is as fulfilling—or more fulfilling—than following a passion. Righting a wrong can become a mission itself, as it has for her twice.

All these women are important guides for me as I figure out where to start and how to become invested in the issues that interest me, and my guess is that you can find similar inspiration in your life. Eleanor Roosevelt is a role model for me in an abstract way, because I can only learn of her actions from historical accounts. I have never met Brené Brown in person, even though we have spoken at the same conference. And Nancy Lublin is a friend and a hero but a woman whose style is very different from mine. You don't have to be in proximity to people to follow their actions, and you don't have to be exactly like them to learn how to start.

ACCEPT THE JOURNEY

Sometimes you get thrown into opportunities to lead, even when you don't want to go there. Nina Klotsman, a friend of a friend, was a fearless woman and activist in Russia, willing to tackle any topic, any task. She worked on a number of projects with the mission to educate and support women in Russia. When she wasn't at work or raising her daughter, she used her time to make meaningful contributions to the women in her community.

Nina's life work was focused on supporting women, and she never imagined that it would be because of breast cancer that she'd leave her mark on the world. But when a group of volunteers from Project Kesher, an organization whose mission it is to support women activists, attended a retreat north of Moscow, the topic of breast-cancer screening and treatment came up. The normally ebullient Nina sat in silence, her hands folded across her chest. It turned out that she was keeping a secret: The previous fall, Nina had felt a lump in her own breast and had done nothing about it.

After the meeting, she mentioned it to Svetlana, one of the group leaders, who urged her to seek medical help immediately. But Nina, an engineer, architect and single mom, said she was too busy—and that she really didn't think she was important enough to get the proper care.

Svetlana was not satisfied and met with the other leaders of the group to come up with a plan to pull Nina forward. Rather than singling her out, they urged all 16 women in the group to get mammograms, offering to pay for everyone's exam. Almost everyone went right away. A number of women found that they had early-stage breast cancer, and all were able to get treatment and move into remission.

But not Nina. She didn't get a mammogram for another six months, and when she finally did go, the news was not good. The cancer was aggressive and invasive. She had a mastectomy, but the cancer had already spread throughout her body and she was told that she had less than a year to live.

Back in the United States, the CEO of Project Kesher, Karyn Gershon, a creative and compassionate woman, refused to accept Nina's fate and the fact that this woman who was so full of life now faced a death sentence. She asked for Nina's medical records and asked another friend who was undergoing breast cancer treatment in the States to ask if her doctor could review them. The doctor contacted Karyn, telling her that a course of treatment was available that was likely to prolong Nina's life by several years—and that it was worth the fight. Aware that she could not afford the treatment, Nina's doctor had not told her about the drug that could help to prolong her life. With this knowledge in hand, the women of Project Kesher once again rallied to find a solution. One of the activists, a breast cancer survivor herself, offered to pay for Nina's treatment throughout the course of her life.

This group of women had buoyed Nina twice, and this encouraged her to become an activist on this topic. She began to travel to cities throughout Russia, speaking openly about her illness and the lack of resources for women with breast cancer, as well as other illnesses prevalent in girls and women. She lived the remaining three years of her life to the fullest.

By putting a face on the disease, she emboldened other breast cancer patients to join the discussion. One of those women created "Five Letters From Larissa," a step-by-step guide to the breast cancer journey, from suspicion to diagnosis to treatment to survival, which tens of thousands of women have since used. Another group of women created peer support groups for breast cancer survivors as a result of Nina's work. They have launched "health days" where women get together to swim or work out and then go to get mammograms together.

Nina's story is the embodiment of the Parlay Effect. Without doubt, Nina's legacy is a testament to her strength. But in her moments of fear and feeling powerless, it was other women who stepped in to fill that void. By banding together, and intentionally choosing to help her, they helped extend her life, allowing her to impact the lives of many others. What started as a death sentence for Nina turned into a meaningful journey that continues to this day with immeasurable benefits for many other women. This is a classic example of the social science we saw in our Parlay Effect research. Nina did not so much choose her path, as find it imposed upon her. But she accepted that journey, and the women who surrounded her helped Nina more than rise to the challenge.

FIND YOUR COMPLEMENTARY STRENGTH: TEAM UP

In Chapter 03, I presented the value of determining your personal strengths and competencies. I recommended using the Gallup's Clifton StrengthsFinder assessment tool, although other validated assessments will give useful results. Regardless of how you come by your particular strengths, you can use this information to form connections with others who have talents complementary to yours. By teaming up and tackling something together, you may be stronger or more effective.

If you have the strength of being an "Activator"—a person whose natural tendency to most challenges is to ask, "When can we start?"—try teaming up with someone who is "Analytical"—whose natural response is to look for proof. It might help to ensure that you go into opportunities thoughtfully, and well-informed. If you are someone with a naturally strong "Belief" system, who feels she knows her values and is focused on executing them, team up with a partner who is strong in "Ideation," someone fascinated with possibilities. The pairing might prompt you to ask healthy questions that increase the relevance and impact of your strong core. There really is no wrong answer in finding someone to make the journey with you, if you can recognize that different approaches and abilities can result in holistic solutions to the issues that you are trying to tackle.

Social science research supports the value of collaborating with people who are different from you in some way. This builds on the self-expansion model, suggesting that you should see people who are different from you not as a threat but as a form of self-expansion. Both people in the partnership report better interactions and feelings of closeness and personal growth. The research showed this to be true across racial, religious and gender differences.

BE BOLD, BE BRAVE

As a woman who had risen to the top in the advertising industry, I found that bonding with other women at my level provided an outlet. We were all experiencing some level of discrimination and imbalance in the workplace, often the result of unconscious (and sometimes conscious) bias. Simply having each other's backs when those things happened allowed us not only to express our frustration, outrage or disappointment in a safe and confidential way, but also to realize that we were not alone. This bonding and understanding of our common experiences gave us the strength to push back, the confidence to stand up for ourselves, and the grounding to validate that what we were experiencing was real. It encouraged us to be brave.

In more recent years, some progressive employers have been trying to formally create forums for women to come together and share their experiences. Yet in many industries, women are still in the minority, and the higher we look up the ladder, the fewer women there are. The rare ones have the guts to be open about what they have faced, risking alienation from their companies and industries in doing so.

Ellen Pao was one such female executive, taking the bold decision to sue her partners in the venture capital firm Kleiner Perkins for discriminating against her. She lost that suit, and has subsequently taken significant flack for speaking up. Susan Fowler, formerly a mid-level software engineer at Uber, is another. She made the bold move to speak up about the rampant sexism that Uber's human resources and executive team had ignored. Susan shed important light on the lack of values-based leadership within her company and the industry, but ended up resigning because she thought that she couldn't change her work environment alone. Susan's courage, however, had tremendous impact. By denouncing the toxic culture at Uber, she set in motion a series of events that ultimately resulted in the ouster of Uber's co-founder and CEO, Travis Kalanick, and the termination of about 20 employees accused of harassment or other issues.

Clearly, speaking up so boldly comes with huge risks. Financially, the chance you may be ousted from a job whose income you depend keeps a lot of us quiet. We just can't risk being fired by bringing up controversial issues or challenging the status quo. From a community or network standpoint, we don't want to be ostracized, so we often keep the inappropriate behavior or discrimination to ourselves. It takes a lot of confidence to rock the boat, especially when you are rocking it alone. What's the upside?

We have now seen the power of the #MeToo movement. Ellen Pao and Susan Fowler fired up a discussion about the treatment of women in the workplace that is building momentum in many industries. We've seen that as women come forward, supported by their private friendships and public allies, they inspire even more women to share their stories. As they step up to allege that they have been exposed to patterns of sexual discrimination, manipulation, bias and even rape by moguls like Gustavo Martinez, the CEO of J. Walter Thompson; Harvey Weinstein of The Weinstein Company, and the actor Bill Cosby, other women are gathering strength to process their own experiences. Some have been bold enough to come forward publicly themselves. Often, the courageous acts of others inspire us to do the same—to find the things that matter to us and spur us into action.

I tried hard to be a champion of women while I was running advertising agencies. But I became a really outspoken advocate after I developed my own platform, which was not dependent on a boss or an employer. There is nothing wrong with taking action when it is slightly less personally risky. Often, you can be more candid and effective after leaving an industry, because you are less concerned about the personal ramifications. After all, we need to protect ourselves while speaking up for others.

TEACH EACH OTHER

Ellen and Susan both set change in motion, change that is clearly being felt across their industries. They are railing against both intentional and unintentional bias, against closed doors that leave us out of key conversations, and against double standards that prevent us from airing our grievances or expressing anger, for fear that we will be misheard or, worse, misrepresented.

Sometimes, though, we are our own worst enemies here. In fact, I have seen self-sabotage occur often in the business world, as well as in the world of philanthropy. I call it the self-fulfilling prophesy of high-achieving women, and it goes like this:

You work exceptionally hard and master key skills. You develop a reputation for being great at what you do. If you are lucky, those contributions are noticed, appreciated and you are rewarded with more responsibility. Of course, you will assume the increased responsibility! You can't drop any balls now. No one else can do your job as well as you, so you do it all. And you resent doing it all—and eventually you burn out.

SO, WHAT'S THE ANSWER?

Protecting our accomplishments often comes at the expense of training the next wave of women to take over for us. Why give assignments to another woman who doesn't have your level of experience or proven ability to deliver? What if she doesn't do it as well as you do? Those are reasonable concerns, and it is understandable to fear that delegating important responsibilities to someone junior to you might result in work that could be less effective than if you had done it yourself.

But if we don't pass on assignments while mentoring, coaching and training the women coming after us, they will miss opportunities to learn and grow. This is where we need to apply the Parlay Effect. #MeToo had ramifications, but it was mostly exposing the negative behavior of men towards women. It's time to create a ripple effect of positive behavior for the next generation.

If we don't do this, we will become bitter, overworked and eventually stifled in our growth, because we are taking on more than we are passing along. If we burn out, another strong woman may not take our place—the opportunity is likely go to a man who thinks he is capable of the job, when he has only 50% of the skills to do it. The onus is on us to pull the next level of women forward. This is true in the world of business, in the world of giving and even in the world of parenting, where we can train our kids to be more helpful, thoughtful and responsible. Doing it all is no longer the path to growth, success and fulfillment. This inability to express vulnerability too often isolates us from those around us. As we learned from Nina's journey, rarely do women go through life without encountering some need for help—and women are the likely candidates to step up in that time of need.

MAKE IT COUNT

Remember Tiffany, the techie filmmaker? As her career progressed, she decided to use both film and technology as vehicles for meaningful social change, producing films that are shown on the Web and intended to drive people to action. She created her film and her movement, called "50/50," based on her revelation that far more women were elected to public office during the last presidential election than we know about, and that we should work toward a time when an equal number of men and women participate in the race. Her film was a great success, showing online and in schools in many communities, stimulating discussion and action.

Her next film, "30,000 Days," made the observation that the average person is on Earth for 30,000 days. It called on viewers to reflect on how to make some sort of impact each day. Expanding on the film, she created an annual international event called Character Day, which is celebrated online, in classrooms and at companies across the United States, in 19 countries and at 130,000 unique events. A number of meaningful actions have grown out of this event: Last year, the event prompted Hong Kong to launch a citywide Cultivating Kindness campaign. The Bahamas helped bring Character Day to all local families, schools and businesses on the islands. The University of Texas at Dallas offered scholarships to students demonstrating tremendous character. Even the Dalai Lama heard about the event and sent a special and supportive message.

This chapter has largely been about taking small steps toward action, using those trial balloons to interact with others and identify what we care about. The key is not to get stuck in the experimentation phase, but to use experimentation to find your passion. Tiffany is an excellent example of how experimenting with her skills and interests led her to make each day count.

10 WAYS TO BRING WOMEN FORWARD

While you are looking for your chances to go broad and then go deep, it's important to be open about your journey, and to share it with others. Too often we prefer not to talk about our successes for fear that others will view us as boastful or self-serving. We don't talk about our failures because we fear that exposing mistakes and weaknesses will leave us vulnerable, opening us to criticism and exclusion.

When we aren't open about our journeys, other women who are looking to us for guidance and direction don't have the chance to benefit from learning of a real woman's experience. Once we can get away from trying to project perfection rather than humanity, we become relatable. And once others can relate to us, the door for mutual learning and collective growth opens.

If you are a "woman of power"—at work, in a community or in your family—looking for ways to be relatable and to pull other women forward is much easier than you think. I'll give you 10 ways to get started:

1. Leave your door open: Try keeping your desk stocked with fruit or snacks as a way to entice people to come in and talk. Approachability is key. Make yourself available to those around you, either literally or figuratively. This will allow women who need help to feel comfortable coming to you. Leaving your door open suggests that you have no secrets and that you have a desire to interact with others. Often, the best results will come from being a good listener in the conversations, rather than trying to impart wisdom off the bat.

2.   Tell her what others won't: As women, one of our greatest strengths is empathy. Yet it can often hold us back. Why? Because it might prevent us from hard conversations that let another woman know that she may not be perceived in the way she wants. No one wants to deliver difficult news, but if it is done in the right way, it is often kinder than avoiding the problem.

Is there a misperception about her that she can address? Are others getting the wrong opinion based on her style or her actions? Is there something she can do to be better received, more relatable or more effective? Does she have broccoli stuck in her teeth? (I joke.) If there is a way to tell her what others won't—something constructive and helpful, delivered in a supportive rather than a critical way, she will appreciate knowing. We women often step lightly around each other rather than give direct insight and feedback that will help make each other successful. How would you like to be told something? I have a dear friend who once said, "Anything can be said, as long as it's said with love." Try expressing your feedback from that vantage point.

3. *Reinforce what she says:* If she is a quiet type, or your environment is one where it's hard to be heard, be the person in the room who reinforces her ideas and publicly gives her credit for them, so no one steals her insights. This will help her build confidence and her credibility. Make sure to repeat to others the insights she has. Expand the number of people who get to hear her contributions or point of view, and refer to her by name—"As Anita said"—and by gesturing toward her so that everyone in the room is reminded who you are talking about. She will feel seen, heard and recognized, and it will prevent a louder and more dominant person from appropriating her ideas.

4. *Mentor in All Directions:* Mentoring has so many meanings. We often mentor people younger and more junior than we are, providing wisdom based on our own life experiences. That is great, but don't stop there. You can also mentor someone older or more advanced in their career than you are. Did such a person grow up pre-technology? Helping her familiarize herself with things she may not know could be a great help. Invite her to an event of your peers so that she can gain insights into a different generation. Mentoring can happen from top down, from young to old, and from peer to peer. Don't be so literal that you miss your chance to help.

5.   Coach Her: Do you remember that great coach in school, your breakthrough yoga instructor or a meaningful teacher who got you to realize your potential? Recognize her "personal best" and key accomplishments, even if they are small steps. Encouraging another woman and cheering her on is often a needed boost. Be her biggest fan in an authentic way, and she will gain confidence in herself.

6.   Pair up: Sometimes, going alone is the hardest part. Suggest that you travel together to an event, so she doesn't have to go in alone. Go with her to an important doctor's appointment and be her second set of ears. Stand by her side when she is advocating for herself or for others. Sit next to her as she makes an important phone call. In stressful situations, one plus one will likely be far more power-ful than two, and often, just being there with her will provide more strength and confidence than you can imagine.

7.   Introduce her around: Perhaps someone other than you can be helpful to many women you know. Help where you can, and when you run out of your reach, introduce her to other great women (and men) with whom she can connect and grow. I met some of my best friends and allies through amazing women who brought us together, and I have seen the effect of connections, opportunities and victories spread out through an outward chain of connections from one woman to the next.

8.   *Share information:* Many of us are over-extended, doing so much that we don't have time to read the fine print or hear the whole story. For many women, being stretched thin also means being out of the loop. If there is information that would be helpful to someone you know—a school event, a meaningful job opportunity, a news article that is of interest to her, or even a suggested attire for an up-coming event—clue her in, so she is involved and prepared.

9.   *Invite and include her:* Whether it's something happening in your industry, your company, your neighborhood or your group of friends, invite her. Being included is key for us to gain validation, exposure and confidence. Being excluded is far more damaging than we imagine. Let her be the one to opt out if something isn't right, rather than failing to offer her the option of joining. Often, being wanted is a significant boost in itself.

10.   *Pass it on:* Many of us do not recognize our own power to help others. If you have followed any of the suggestions above, you will know how good you feel in helping someone else succeed. If you have a friend who is frustrated by the roadblocks around her, unfulfilled in some of her daily tasks, or somehow yearning for a way to feel that she is having an impact, remind her of her power to pull other women forward. Then encourage her to do so!

The process of helping to reach out to another woman, and encouraging the next woman to do that for someone else is the beginning of the Parlay Effect: the trackable moments when we start waves of empowerment that turn into action. It's our ticket to having an impact, to independence and connection. We don't need to rely on others to boost us, because we become capable of doing it for ourselves, and more importantly, for another woman as well. One becomes two, and pretty soon our results reach thousands of women who will benefit.

QUESTIONS TO ASK, STEPS TO TAKE:

This chapter has been all about taking some action, small as it may be. You don't need to predetermine what the action will be, but rather simply to start somewhere. Ask yourself these questions to get you going:

- Is there something that you excel at—a specific skill you have—that can be put to use for the benefit of others?

- Is there a family tradition that might guide your first foray into helping others, much as was the case with Tiffany?

- Can you think of someone you admire for her actions, and can you envision yourself walking in her footsteps?

- In the spirit of launching "trial balloons," can you list five to 10 things that you'd like to try just to test the waters?

For some people, simply getting off the couch is difficult in itself. If you identify with this hurdle, but truly want to start some new action in your life, try this:

1. Identify a problem. Figure out what you really care about. What gets you angry or feels really unfair to you? Experiencing an injustice of some sort often inspires action, especially for those who may other-

wise feel shy about stepping out. Sometimes, when the stakes are high enough, taking action is the only option.

2.   Find a partner. We often need encouragement, which is where the buddy system can be helpful. Ideally, you want to find someone who cares about what you do, but who might approach it slightly differently. By now, you have probably identified areas in which you hold competencies and strengths. It's best now to find someone who complements you, rather than doubling up. This way, you can lean on each other through the hard stretches, and challenge each other to see things differently as well.

The most important message here is to start small and not get too caught up in expectations of what will happen down the line. See where things lead, and respond accordingly.

CHAPTER 08

ACTIVATE CASCADES OF CHANGE

You may not always have a comfortable life and you will not always be able to solve all of the world's problems at once, but don't ever underestimate the importance you can have, because history has shown us that courage can be contagious and hope can take on a life of its own.

— MICHELLE OBAMA

IT'S EXCEPTIONALLY DIFFICULT TO TRACK THE PARLAY Effect, the "thing after the thing" that shows our exponential impact on others. I can think of many examples of people who set positive experiences in motion for others, but their actual impact is extraordinarily difficult to measure. Take the elderly man at our local park, for example. He is there, like clockwork, every morning at 7:30 a.m., doing tai chi in the corner of the green where the bikers, runners and dog walkers stream by. He greets each of us, every time, looking us in the eye, nodding and wishing us each a "Nice day" (or a "good day" or a "great day"). It's obvious from watching him that some of the park's regulars look forward to seeing him, and even have their own greeting for him as they pass by. They call out, "Good morning!" or "Looking good!" or "Have a great day too," variations of cheery exchanges to start the day. Beyond these brief interactions, who knows whether these expressions of goodwill extend beyond the park when these people arrive at their jobs, homes and communities? The cascade effect is untrackable, but I know that for me, being greeted by a happy stranger leaves me feeling more upbeat. And I carry that with me.

In earlier chapters, I chronicled evidence of this cascade of good. We met Julie Abrams, who would never have guessed that the love she showed for her young neighbor, Carmina, would have left such an imprint on her that Carmina would carry forward the lessons she taught her to her own children more than a decade later. We heard about how one phone call between two young women halfway around the world helped change the trajectory for Sreileak Hour, who will become a force of change in Cambodia. And we followed my sister Rachel in her Letter Farmer van, who through the simple act of letter-writing is bringing friends and families back together.

Despite this handful of examples of setting change into motion, we often can't exactly calculate the multiplier effect. We don't always know whether those who have received an uplifting message will continue the chain. But I believe that in the majority of cases, it does carry forward.

I say this from personal experience. When I founded Parlay House, initially a gathering of just 20 women, I had no idea it would grow into a connected group of women thousands strong—in cities across the globe. The genesis was this: one woman inviting another woman to join her in an experience. Yet it turned into something so much more.

One might say that the growth of an organization is not proof of a cascade of good but rather a cascade of relevance. Parlay House struck a chord with women. As the founder, once the women left "the parlor," I often did not hear any more of what ensued. Apart from the activities of RE Group (discussed in Chapter 06) and other smaller groups of women that have formed to support each other as a result of their Parlay experience, I am not party to the conversations that happen after an event. I am not an audience to the anticipation of the next event, where one woman has sensed that another friend, colleague, sister, mother, daughter or aunt would also enjoy becoming part of the group. All I know is that our members asked us to add another woman to our list and introduced her to everyone else when she arrived at Parlay House.

Of course, Parlay House is not the only answer for creating societal change, connection and meaning. The trick is to get beyond transactions and into relating at a deeper level. It's not the tracking or the accounting that drives the cascade. It happens at the level of feeling.

THE TRANSFER OF MONEY

The most obvious way to initiate a transfer of good is through a traditional path, the transfer of money—charity in its most recognized form. Giving money is synonymous with charity. For many of us, it is the first thought when the topic turns to personal generosity. But look a little farther, and it becomes obvious that people give more freely in some situations than others. In a study conducted by the Department of Social and Decision Sciences at Carnegie Mellon University and reported in *The Guardian,* Deborah Small and a group of researchers showed that people are decidedly more generous about helping someone when they know the recipients or details about their situation. "In a series of experiments, it was found that people are much more responsive to charitable pleas that feature a single, identifiable beneficiary than they are to statistical information about the scale of the problem being faced," they wrote.

This conclusion was based on a number of scientific experiments. In their first laboratory study of people's willingness to make a charitable donation, the researchers learned that subjects were more willing to give money to other people who had lost money when they could verify that the loss had occurred. If they were told that people *would* be losing money (in the near future), they were far less likely to donate. Perhaps they thought that the bad event might not happen and that their donation would not be put to good use, or for the use it was intended. A second study asked people to give money to a family in need. The research found that people were far more likely to give money to a specific family who had been vouched for as needy and who had already been selected from a list. They were less likely to give to a family that had not yet been specifically selected.

Small attributes this change in generosity to the distinction between identifiable victims—humans who need immediate help—and unspecified people in need. They applied the results of this study to charities focused on the idea of prevention, rather than the treatment of immediate problems. As they put it, "When Jessica McClure ('Baby Jessica') was trapped in a well in Texas, over $700,000 was sent to her family for the rescue effort. If those donations had instead been spent on preventative health care for children, hundreds of children's lives could potentially have been saved"—as compared with the single one. What this says is that our choices about how and when to be generous with our cash are driven by human stories. The givers can identify with an immediate and specific situation and respond based on their desire to help.

The study also showed that the willingness to be generous not only increased with knowledge of the victim but also based on the knowledge that other donors had already given. Reputable sources, not just our friends and families, can influence us here. The *Guardian* article revealed that donors to an international development charity were more likely to respond to a match-funding campaign if they knew that the match came from a lead donor with a strong reputation, for example, the Bill and Melinda Gates Foundation, than if it came from an anonymous source. Leadership gifts through the Gates Foundation, for instance, made the giving more credible and gave a sense of impact through numbers. "The good news is that charitable giving is contagious—seeing others give makes an individual more likely to give, and gentle encouragement from a prominent person in your life can make also make a big difference to your donation decisions—more than quadrupling them."

Habit also plays a part. Those who made a habit of volunteering were more likely to donate their time again than those who had never volunteered before. Getting over the hump the first time was more difficult than repeating the action.

REFRAMING GENEROSITY

Sean Stannard-Stockton, writing in the *Stanford Social Innovation Review,* frames "generous and giving" behavior in a different way: He links the generosity not to altruism and charity in the strictest sense, but to our desire to contribute to a real community. Stockton notes that Merriam-Webster's Dictionary defines altruism as "unselfish regard for or devotion to the welfare of others" and also as "behavior by an animal that is not beneficial to or may be harmful to itself but that benefits others of its species." He goes on to say, however: "But I believe that only an incredibly narrow view of life holds that helping others is somehow separate from helping ourselves. Humans are communal animals. Without 'others,' we find life intolerable. If a person sacrifices for another, it is not simply 'unselfish,' it is because they would be completely miserable if they chose to look the other way. Any parent knows that the happiness and health of their children is more important than their own needs…that humans are hard-wired to enjoy the act of helping others. Feeling happy and good about helping others is a sign of positive mental health."

Stockton also points out that he sees very little evidence that people give in expectation of getting something in return: the boomerang effect of charity. This brings us once again to the idea of reframing reciprocity as giving to a broader spectrum of society and having the effects reverberate outward. It is not so much about expecting that giving will come back to us in a beneficial way but the pure pleasure of doing good for someone else.

I have come around to this reframed notion of giving in my philanthropic life, specifically to:

1. Find ways to identify with another person.

2. Give in order to open the door to others, who gain confidence by following your lead.

3. Give without thought of return. You are then freed from the potential disappointment of those who do not behave reciprocally.

Through this lens, giving of my time, ideas and even money becomes so much clearer.

THE VALUE OF ACTS

Charitable giving through a donation is probably the quickest way to give. It can be meaningful even in very small amounts. Take the story of my chance connection with a young girl named Jordan. It all started when my dog and I walked (yet again) through the local park, waving at the man doing tai chi. As we walked, I came across a small, embroidered purse lying in the street. It looked dry and clean, as if it hadn't been there long. I picked it up and looked inside, finding $40 in cash and a school ID card; nothing pointed to the age of the owner, but I did find a home address. I could only imagine one of my daughters losing her purse and ID and how badly she would feel, so I popped it in the mail, tucking in an extra $20 as a surprise gift for its recipient. Knowing that the loss of the purse had probably created a lot of stress, I hoped to modestly compensate for that loss.

A week later, I received a note in the mail:

Dear Mrs. Devereux-Mills,
My name is Jordan. I am the owner of the purse you found and
mailed back to me. I had lost it on a school field trip to San

Francisco. From that experience, I learned a lot about simple human kindness. From my friends who were willing to help me pay for our mandatory dinner out in the city, to receiving the purse in the mail, I found just how caring and kind people will be, even to a random stranger. I will remember this experience for a long time to come and this amazing global community of people who care. Thank you so much for being such an incredible person who has inspired me to go beyond obligation.

Who was this girl? What could I find out about her? Did this cascade of kindness continue? I looked for her on Facebook and found nothing. Then I searched Google and found an article from three years earlier about a 9-year-old girl who was the youngest swimmer ever to complete "Escape from Alcatraz," a one-and-a-half-mile swim that she did to raise money for mosquito nets in Uganda. The world works in strange ways. I, too, have a connection to Uganda. It was in Uganda that I helped start a school that serves children who lost their parents to malaria or AIDS. So, I wrote back to Jordan to see what other ways our lives intersected. It turned out that she is a gymnast, as I had been in school. She hoped to be a writer one day, and I am now an author.

We never talked about the $20 I put into her purse, and my thought was that she might not have remembered how much she originally had. But then I got another note from her:

…When I received my purse back from you, I found $20 in it that I was unsure if I put in. It is possible that I put it in for spending money on my trip, but I was not fully sure. Instead of keeping it, I donated it to Nothing but Nets on Triple Day— they triple your donation when you donate, so it was like do-

nating $60. I chose NBN for that particular donation because it is a charity where a little goes a long way. In most charities it requires many donations to make a difference, but $10 can save a child's life in Nothing but Nets.

I did something for her, and she decided, without prompting, to pass it on to children who might not have been as fortunate as she. And she did it in a way that multiplied the cash value.

I am relatively certain that Jordan did not just choose to pass along her $20 without having been exposed to giving in the past. From what I can tell, her parents and role models believe in the practice of giving. What wonderful circumstances and lessons for us all: We can model best practices so those that follow us learn to behave in the same way. Sounds like a game-changing activity to me.

But what if you are not brought up in a household or a community that models giving?

EACH ONE, TEACH ONE

My dear friend Mimi Silbert founded Delancey Street in San Francisco in 1971. The organization directly addresses people leaving prison with nowhere to go, except to return to the streets. They receive no meaningful training or retraining for jobs (or for life) while in prison, and no reliable way to re-enter society. These people, for the most part, did not have parents or people in their lives modeling behavior or best practices for them. Delancey Street provides not only a place to live post-incarceration; it provides the first real and supportive living community that many of these people has ever known.

What started as a single residential facility in San Francisco now operates in seven cities nationally and serves over 2,000 people at a time. In expanding the organization, Mimi has no hired or "paid" staff, only the "former inmates" who come to live and train at each facility. Each location has a number of businesses, like a restaurant, an auto repair shop, a picture framer, a moving company, Christmas tree lots and more. Those profitable businesses generate the income that the organization uses to operate.

It all works because of the basic operating principle at Delancey Street: "Each one, teach one," which empowers every person living at a facility to become a teacher, the expert who must pass along the information for the next person taking over their job.

If you are fortunate enough to make it into a Delancey Street program, you arrive at the facility prepared to start your life with a completely clean slate, and you take the available entry-level job within the facility. The person training you will be someone who, like you, came fresh out of prison and who has just learned the ropes of your job in the months before you arrived. In training you, they become the teacher, finding validation and confidence at having developed skills and knowledge at a level that they can train the next person coming along. When it's time for a job shift, they take on a new role, and are trained by the person who came before them. Everyone is learning. Everyone is teaching. Everyone is rising. It is all based on the understanding of teamwork, and the insight that if the most junior person doesn't succeed, it eats away at the foundation of the organization and pulls everyone else down.

As the newly trained members of the Delancey Street community build the solid foundation that allows them to graduate from the program and leave the residential facility, they become roommates with former Delancey residents who have transitioned into the general population. These people keep pulling each other forward, often for years, creating a chain of success that provides strength to the individuals and true value to the communities. It's an example of a clear cascade of change, a chain reaction that passes on through the organization where one becomes two, then three and so on.

But what about examples that amount to more than one plus one plus one, and are exponential in their impact?

Christopher Bergland, author of *The Athlete's Way,* writes in an article in *Psychology Today* that some people are naturally wired to be more empathetic than others. If you are someone who has that gift, exercising that compassion comes more easily to you. But he also notes that if you are not naturally wired this way, it can be learned: "Because our brain's neural circuitry is malleable and can be rewired through neuroplasticity, one's tendency for empathy and compassion is never fixed. We all need to practice putting ourselves in someone else's shoes to reinforce the neural networks that allow us to 'Love thy neighbor as thyself' and 'Do unto others as you would have them do unto you.'"

Studies on neuroplasticity, which is the brain's ability to change and form new neural connections, have shown the possibility of establishing new behavior over the course of our lives. Plasticity-based therapies currently in development treat not only a wide spectrum of cognitive problems but also give us hope that, with some effort, changing certain orientations and patterns is available to everyone. Even the act of learning a new skill, ballroom dancing, for example, can open up and alter pathways in the brain. This means we can learn to overcome and become in ways we did not think were previously possible. It also means we can learn to give—and love to give—in ways we may not previously have thought of.

Other approaches can help with this as well, simply by introducing something new. Here are some suggested ways to open yourself up:

1. Slow down

People often react quickly, making knee-jerk choices with little thought. Slowing down to process situations and other people's stories allows you to internalize them, and as a result, relate to them and become more connected.

2. Avoid projecting your own experiences onto others

Since no two people have lived identical lives or had parallel experiences, you cannot assume that others will feel the way you do— or need what you might need in any situation.

3. Put yourself in the shoes of the next person

If you can imagine the experience of another, you can anticipate what he or she might feel, see and need, even if your personal situations are dramatically different.

These are examples of what Bergland points to as LKM (loving-kindness meditation), a practice of meditating that can actually rewire your brain. It starts with simply taking a few minutes each day to "quietly and systematically" contemplate the needs of others who are suffering (including yourself).

ONE BECOMES SEVEN

One of the more extraordinary cases of stepping into someone else's shoes is the story of Richard Branson. Famous for doing everything in a big way, Branson is founder of Virgin Megastores, Virgin Records, Virgin Airways and Virgin Group, which consists of more than 400 other companies. Not only is Branson an innovator and rule-breaker, but he is also a world record holder several times over, including for making a trans-Atlantic flight in a hot-air balloon. More recently, his focus has shifted to helping to save the planet, with global initiatives that cover everything from wildlife and land preservation to developing new environmentally friendly fuels.

Branson is a well-known philanthropist, and it would surprise no one to hear about his generous acts. But when asked for an example of the cascade of change in his own life, he responded with a story not about large grants or global foundations, but rather about a small gesture on his part that resulted from one woman's courage to ask for help (in this way, men too participate in the Parlay Effect).

A few years ago, while Branson was on a trip to his South African game reserve, he was approached by a woman who had worked for him for years on his large local staff. He knew her, but he did not know her well. Still, she stood beside him at the entrance to the park, and she spoke. Her voice was steady, resolute, poised. If she had any reservations about approaching Branson, she bottled them up and spoke with confidence and utter determination that he support her request. She asked him whether he might be able to spare $300 so that she could buy a sewing machine. And with that sewing machine she could support her family in a really meaningful way. Branson rarely carries cash, but that day he dug into his pocket and found that he had the $300 she was asking for. He gave it to the woman, who accepted it gratefully.

Six months later, he returned to South Africa and was greeted by two other women, who presented him with an extraordinary cloak. It had been made on the very sewing machine bought with the money he had given to the woman who had stepped forward. When Branson asked where the woman was, the two others responded, smiling. They told him that she was too busy at the market to come and see him at the moment. Her business was booming. In fact, six of them now work for her, and are all able to help support their families.

The bold request of this one woman yielded the sewing machine that cascaded into the employment of seven women and dramatically improved living conditions for many more. What was only pocket money to Richard Branson changed one life, then seven, then the lives of those in the village, having an impact that continues to spread outward to this day.

START YOUR OWN CASCADE

You've learned in this book about the acts of others, both big and small, that have contributed to sustainable change. Whether you are bold enough to take a bit of luck and pass it on to others like the woman on Richard Branson's game reserve, or generous in a way that takes generosity and creates a multiplier effect like Jordan, or nurturing enough to not only practice empathetic behavior but to also model it for others, like Julie, you are becoming a crucial part of a cascade of change. And that change is happening now. From the

#MeToo to the #TimesUp movements, women are lending strength to others in inspiring and empowering ways. A palpable sense of forward movement is building; and yet there is also the danger that that it will slow or stop. These fires of passion and fury tend to flicker out. Bad guys come back with their sins forgotten or forgiven. The progress fades unless we take this time to show our strength and keep the momentum going.

The Parlay Effect happens based on a whole series of events that are triggered by:

* our anger and outrage
* our feeling and empathizing
* our trusting and sharing
* our emulating and inspiring
* our similarities found within our differences
* our choice to pull another woman forward.

Please join us. We need your strength.

CREATING SUPPORTIVE COMMUNITIES FOR WOMEN

My y lifetime listens to yours.

— MURIEL RUKEYSER

I HAVE A PERSONAL SAYING THAT GOES LIKE THIS: "We are stronger when we are connected." This is what inspired me to create the community of Parlay House. It taught me that the company of other women helps me to feel grounded, fulfilled and empowered. It has been a joy to see the membership grow over time, knowing that other women feel the same way.

My desire is for these communities of women to continue to spread, and for the numbers to grow month by month, year by year. If you live anywhere close to where one of our chapters is located, please consider this an invitation to join us. If you don't live in the San Francisco, Oakland, New York City, London, Los Angeles, Boston, Washington D.C., Atlanta (or close to a Parlay House chapter in a city that is soon to launch), or if the topics we choose to discuss aren't ones that resonate with you, don't despair. The great news is that there is no limit on the number of supportive communities.

If you need a boost to get started creating your own community, I'd like to share some core principles that were integral to making Parlay House work:

- *Gather at home*

Opening your house or apartment and welcoming people in is a special gesture. That act in and of itself is symbolic. Hosting strangers, new acquaintances and friends in the place where we live is the beginning of an openness and transparency that sets the stage for meaningful dialogue and exchange. And if no one has a home that is convenient for a broad range of people, find a local business, restaurant or gathering space where a group of near-strangers can feel safe and comfortable.

- *Ensure diversity from the start*

As with every living organism, growth starts with a single cell. By nature, people tend to bring other people who are like themselves, so if you can start with a range of women from different backgrounds, the group will continue to be interesting, varied and diverse as the organization grows. Think of diversity in terms of ethnicity, age, sexual orientation, education, success, religion, culture and more.

- *Create an inclusive process*

Parlay House grows as each member takes responsibility for bringing a new member to an event, introducing her, letting her know how it works and making her feel comfortable. Each member gets to choose whether the topic of the month interests her and whether she wants to be there. Allowing for inclusion and self-determination helps to ensure that events are successful, because the attendees want to be there and are already interested in the topic.

- *Make it affordable*

Pampering our members, who are usually the ones pampering others, has been key to our success. The pampering thus far has included champagne and munchies. But we do the math, figuring out how to buy or make the food and drinks so that the ticket prices (from $20 to $30 for the most part) can be afforded by all. This is crucial to creating a flat organization where everyone is equal and there are no haves and have-nots. Typically, the gatherings are sized in a way that fills the space in order to create energy without being uncomfortable. We have about 70 people at each event in San Francisco, and closer to 40 in some of the other cities. If you want a spread that costs more than what it would take to keep ticket prices accessible, consider BYO, finding a local supplier who wants to sponsor the event or making a potluck a part of the evening.

Even if you are someone who can afford to be a sponsor of events, it is important that each person pay their share to attend. We have found that when events are free, those who come do not have enough at stake in the process and tend to devalue what you are providing. They say they will come and then fail to show up because they lose nothing by doing so. A lot is lost by the host, on the other hand, who has either had to say "no" to another woman or who ends up with lots of leftovers because of no-shows.

- *Be smart with your wait list*

If your events are as popular as ours, you are likely to max out and need to create a wait list. In order to perpetuate the philosophy of one woman supporting the next one, we ask that women who cancel donate their ticket to the next woman on the wait list, creating another chain reaction of support.

- *Don't talk Shop*

At Parlay House events, we feel that it's important to stay away from work as a frame of reference. There are many career-related support networks, which are crucial as we women make our way to the top. But there are very few safe spaces to talk about the other things—the often unacknowledged and unspoken truths that connect us. Be really clear in framing the conversation that the emphasis should be on getting to know each other as women, not as workers. "What we do" should not substitute for "who we are." With a diverse range of participants, everyone will appreciate being seen in a way that highlights who she is and what she cares about rather than defining her by a title or achievements.

- *Create a space of trust*

Despite its name, which can suggest a reference to gambling, Parlay House has little in common with Las Vegas. But as in Vegas, what happens at Parlay House stays at Parlay House. While we occasionally gather and share quotes from our speakers that have global relevance and meaning, it is important that all the confidential and intimate conversations, experiences and truths people exchange do not become public. In creating a private space, our members are willing to share things that they have rarely or never discussed. Having a place where this is possible is freeing and often cathartic.

The second piece of this "space of trust" is that members are not allowed to come to the event in order to ask something of another member. That means that women who are starting organizations cannot come with the intention of asking another member to help, for example, with marketing or to donate to a cause. If everyone can participate without worrying that someone will try to extract something from them, they can relax from the get-go.

To be candid, at every single event, the connections and conversations that take place ultimately result in someone donating, helping, volunteering, hiring, referring or connecting afterward. That happens as a result of our gathering and connecting. It's an expression of the Parlay Effect, for sure. But devoting the time when everyone is present to really getting to know one another means that we are heard, seen and understood while we are together. The transactional support can happen later for anyone who finds a reason to carry a new relationship to another level.

- *Be consistent*

Surprise, surprise. We are creatures of habit. We have found that members find great comfort in knowing how most events will unfold. So determine the timing and flow that work for everyone and stick to it. In San Francisco, we find that street parking spaces open up at 6 p.m. and that many of our members want to get home to family by 8:30 p.m., so events run from 6 to 8:30 p.m. Because Mondays and Fridays are busier than midweek, we target Tuesday through Thursdays for events, to get as many people there as possible. New Yorkers tend to work later, so we start later there. The traffic in Los Angeles is horrible during the week, so we have experimented with a Saturday afternoon gathering.

Regardless of time and location, there is a reliable flow for each evening, starting with social (and food) time; a featured speaker, panel or topic; a question-and-answer period, and time at the end to talk with each other about what we have just experienced and learned. When everyone knows the flow and what to expect, we reduce the number of late-comers or midcourse interruptions, and it enhances the experience for everyone.

- *Offer a variety of content*

The consistent feature of every talk, panel, speaker and performance at Parlay House is authenticity. We bring in people who are willing to "get real" and to talk about their struggles as well as their triumphs, insights, mistakes, regrets and revelations. But with that as a guide, we really try to mix up content. Some events are personal stories, others are educational, creative or inspirational. Some people are well-known and some are people you have never heard of.

The advantage of an opt-in, self-selecting membership and range of topics covered is that women choose to come when a subject intrigues them. That means they are naturally more interested and engaged, and that the event is far more likely to be viewed as relevant and meaningful. It sets us up for success.

YOUR PARLAY HOUSE IS A BEGINNING, NOT AN END

Most women who come to events do so to form real and meaningful connections with other women. We get the conversation started, but in a packed room that includes time to listen to a speaker, there is never enough time to really get to know each other. We encourage women who meet each other and feel some sort of spark to take those conversations to the next level by meeting outside Parlay House. Some choose to grab coffee, others participate in a shared experience together, and a third group sets off on some sort of project or endeavor. There is no right or wrong next step, but the idea is to take a next step with at least one new woman.

IN CLOSING ... AND OPENING

There is much potential, strength and fulfillment available to us when we create a cascade effect from one woman to the next. By parlaying outward, we begin to put firm limits on transactional relationships laden with the baggage of expectations and obligations. We open up possibilities that are too big to be accounted for, tracked and measured. They get to the heart of who we are, how we behave, and how we are willing to give something of ourselves for the sake of another. The Parlay Effect is all about this outward-spinning cycle. If we can get to know each other better and appreciate the value of self, we can ultimately apply our self-knowledge in small ways to create meaning for others.

Remember, we all stumble, every one of us. That's why it's a comfort to go hand in hand.

— EMILY KIMBROUGH

ACKNOWLEDGMENTS

YEARS AGO, AFTER MY FIRST AGENT WAS UNSUCCESSFUL in selling my book, Leslie Ziegler Schrock created a hardback of my original draft to encourage me and to keep me going. Her support powers me to this day. Along the way, there have been so many contributors, guides, advisers, supporters and champions who helped me bring this book to life. I am grateful to them all.

In the early days, Sam Horn and Rebecca Zweig shaped my thought process and taught me both structure and substance. Then Cari Guittard infused the work with feisty passion (and chocolate). Alicia Simons and Erica Heilman were instrumental in making the work professional and comprehensive. Divina Infusino brought late-stage insight and Allison Monaghan McGuire helped me extend my voice. And in the final stretch, Rachel Lehmann-Haupt deftly orchestrated the dream team of Peggy Northrop, Ed Windels, Tom Joyce, Nikki McDonald, Lauren Devereux-Burns and Vicky Elliott, who turned the manuscript into its final, beautiful and creative form.

The Parlay Effect would have lacked a critical element without the unique and proprietary work that Serena Chen and I did together. She is a scientist with a loving heart and a truly rare person. She would agree that neither of us could have gotten through all of the programming and analysis without the support of the graduate student Stephen Antonoplis.

What would the Parlay Effect be without my dear friends who created connections for me when I first moved to San Francisco and knew no one? They are the ones who introduced me to the early members of Parlay House. It was those women who lit the fuse of what continues to be a thriving global organization driven by engaged and engaging women who believe in the power of authentic conversation, diversity and inclusion.

Keith Berwick, my inspirational mentor, took a chance by making me part of the Aspen Institute's Henry Crown Fellowship. Participating was pivotal; it infused me with confidence as a values-based leader and made me determined to lead a life of meaning.

In the end, I would not be where I am without the infusion of love from my family. My parents, Gene and Liz Brandzel, raised three strong daughters and gave us permission to be ourselves in the truest possible way. My sisters, Rachel Brandzel Weil and Susan Brandzel are confidantes and champions, making me feel lucky that I was born into sisterhood with them. My daughters, Lauren Devereux-Burns and Ciara Devereux provide me with unbreakable bonds of mutuality, inspiration and love. We have been through so much together, and come out stronger and more connected every time. William and Hans Mills welcome me into their lives as step-mom, and that means a lot. Patrick Burns, my son-in-law, is family in every sense of the word, validating the adage that the family you choose can be as connected and meaningful as the family you are born into. Finally, it was my husband, David, who sat with me through what was, who walks by my side through each day, and without whom I couldn't imagine life.

ABOUT THE AUTHOR

ANNE DEVEREUX-MILLS SPENT THE FIRST HALF OF HER career building and running advertising agencies in New York City as chairman and CEO. When she found herself facing the triple threat of a recurrence of cancer, an empty nest and an unexpected job loss, she took time to reassess her career trajectory and to reconsider the priorities in her life. In 2012, long before the #MeToo movement, she founded Parlay House, a series of salon-style gatherings that now includes over 5,000 women across the United States, Europe and the Middle East. Parlay House's objective is to provide thought-provoking content and a safe space where women can have intimate and authentic conversations that don't happen in other aspects of their lives. It also offers them a way to make meaningful connections with other women outside their traditional social circles, whether personal or professional.

Anne's commitment to issues related to inclusion and empowerment runs deep. Beyond Parlay House, she is a mentor for SHE-CAN, an organization that was founded to support the next generation of women destined to become leaders of countries that have suffered genocide. An activist on issues related to social justice, Anne was a key member of the team that helped pass California's Proposition 36, which brought fair sentencing to thousands of nonviolent inmates as part of California's reform of its three-strikes law. Following the success of this initiative, she was the executive director for the Emmy-nominated documentary film *The Return,* and is working as executive director on two additional films, *Mississippi Red* and *The Green Dress.* Anne supported Stanford University by serving as the executive director of its Healthy Body Image Programs.

Prior to her philanthropic ventures, Anne was chief integration officer at the advertising agency BBDO and managing director of its highly successful health care unit. She then became chairman and CEO of LLNS (the former Lyons Lavey Nickel Swift) and TBWA\WorldHealth. She also served as CEO of Consumer Healthworks, a division of Merkley + Partners, as well as president of Harrison and Star. Anne also helped launch the i.HUG Foundation, a not-for-profit school in Uganda supporting some of that nation's most needy children.

A 2003 Henry Crown Fellow of the Aspen Institute and a member of the Aspen Global Leadership Network, Anne has been honored by a range of organizations, including SHE-CAN, Advertising Women of New York, the All-Stars Foundation, Project Kesher and Worldwide Women.

You can find out more about Parlay house and contact Anne at: www.annedevereuxmills.com.

Made in the USA
Monee, IL
01 October 2021